INC.

CALIF.

STUDIO 4

Thursday
June
27
1968

Show Time
8:00 PM

GUESTS
SHOULD
ARRIVE
7:00 PM

363

ELVIS

'68 COMEBACK

A NOTE FROM THE BOOK'S PRODUCER

In 1968 I was a college student at UCLA and launching my own short-lived music career when Elvis Presley was staging what would be a spectacular comeback. Even as a nineteen-year-old mediocre songwriter and even-less-talented singer, I understood, from a business perspective, the magnitude of what was happening.

Not only was Elvis one of the most profound cultural icons of the twentieth century, he unwittingly paved the way for reinvention and comeback. I'm honored to partner with the brilliantly talented and highly respected Emmy Award–winning director/producer Steve Binder in helping him put together this evergreen book and its extensions, commemorating the Elvis Comeback.

This book is a true insight into the making of the iconic Comeback Special, which became a turning point in Elvis's career, to the public for now and generations to come.

— Spencer Proffer,
Media Producer, Meteor 17

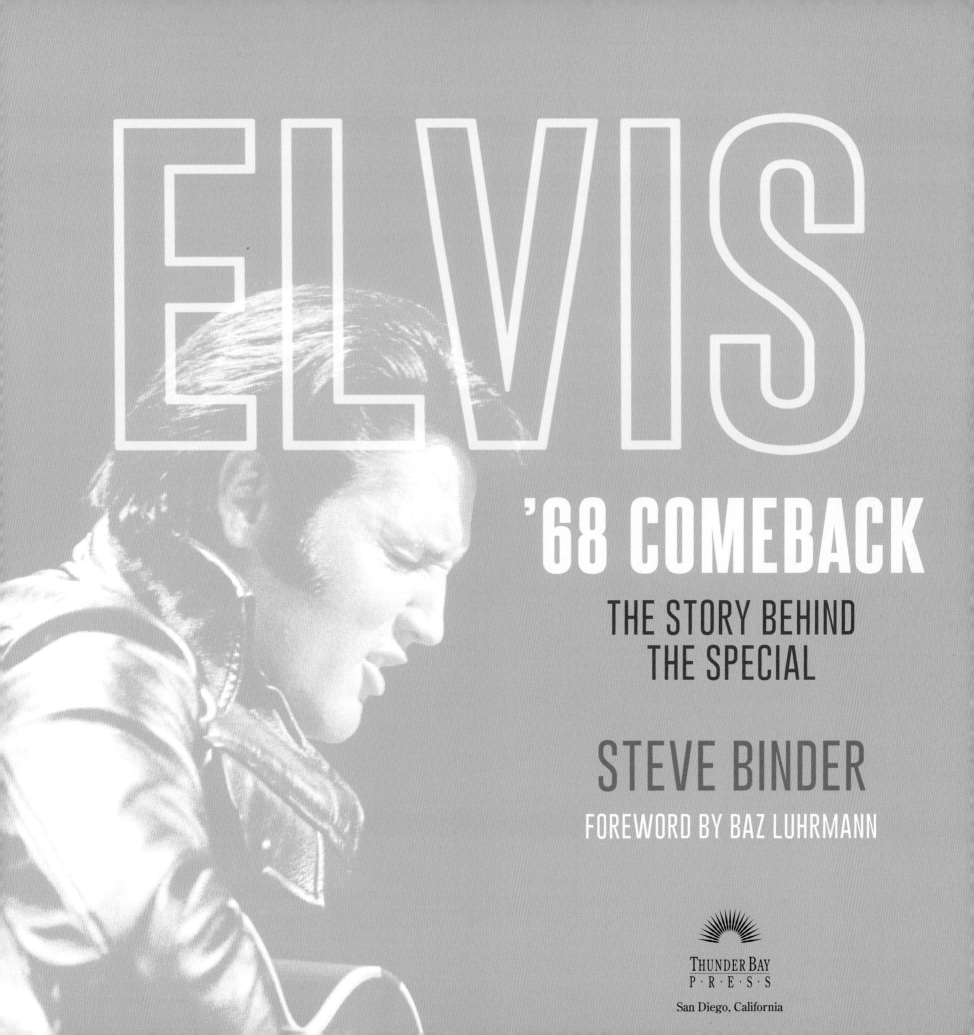

ELVIS

'68 COMEBACK

THE STORY BEHIND
THE SPECIAL

STEVE BINDER

FOREWORD BY BAZ LUHRMANN

THUNDER BAY
P·R·E·S·S

San Diego, California

Thunder Bay Press
An imprint of Printers Row Publishing Group
9717 Pacific Heights Blvd, San Diego, CA 92121
www.thunderbaybooks.com • mail@thunderbaybooks.com

Copyright © 2021 Elvis CB Book, LLC

Meteor 17 Books paperback edition 2018

Printers Row Publishing Group is a division of Readerlink Distribution Services, LLC.
Thunder Bay Press is a registered trademark of Readerlink Distribution Services, LLC.

Correspondence regarding the content of this book should be sent to Thunder Bay Press, Editorial Department, at the above address. Author, illustration, and rights inquiries should be addressed to Elvis CB Book, LLC, 17020 Rancho Street, Encino, CA 91316, Attn: Spencer Proffer, Managing Member.

Thunder Bay Press
Publisher: Peter Norton • Associate Publisher: Ana Parker
Art Director: Charles McStravick
Senior Developmental Editor: April Graham
Editor: Stephanie Romero Gamboa
Production Team: Mimi Oey, Rusty von Dyl

Art Direction and Book Design: Hugh Syme, www.hughsyme.com
Cover Design: Charles McStravick

All black-and-white photography, documents, and original notes courtesy of Steve Binder.
Original notes appear in Steve Binder's handwriting.
Western Recorders photography by George Rodriguez.
Sketches and stage design courtesy of and copyright Gene McAvoy.

Library of Congress Control Number: 2021930581

ISBN: 978-1-64517-673-2

Printed in China

26 25 24 23 22   2 3 4 5 6

It was time for Elvis to do something in a big way.

Steve Binder came at that right time.

And magic happened. Their journey made history.

And still, today, we enjoy and are mesmerized by that magic.

Priscilla Presley

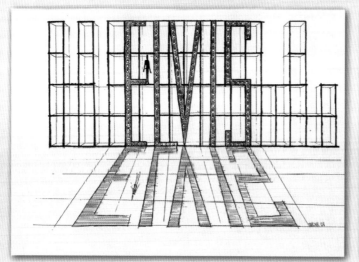
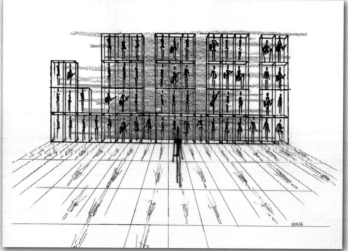

Original sketches of the stage set design for the TV special by Art Director Gene McAvoy

	Foreword from Baz Luhrmann	viii
	Preface	ix
	Acknowledgments	xi
	About the Author	xiii
1	Elvis, the Colonel, and the Snowmen's League	1
2	Setlists, Salaries, and Just Elvis	15
3	Promises Broken	21
4	Pre-Production	29
5	Press Conference	43
6	The Production	47
7	The Arena	61
8	Acoustic / Improv	71
9	Western Recorders	129
10	If I Can Dream	139
11	Saying Goodbye	145
	Post-Special	153
	Epilogue	157
	Recording Sessions	163

In researching the life of Elvis Presley, I have spoken to so many of those who studied, worked with, knew, and loved Elvis, both the person and the iconic entertainer. While everyone has their own particular story of Elvis, one of the essential chapters in the telling of Elvis Presley's life is the story of *Elvis*, the 1968 NBC special.

This is not the place to go into detail as to how a boy from a dirt-poor background found himself channeling an extraordinary new form of music. But once he met the legendary ex-carny and his soon-to-be manager, Colonel Tom Parker (who, as I like to say, was never a colonel, never a Tom, never a Parker), Elvis exploded into the "Atomic Powered Singer" and, seemingly overnight, changed the course of popular youth culture, shaking the very foundations of 1950s America. Almost as suddenly as he rose, he suffered a series of tragedies: the loss of his first love; the dissolution of his band; the death of his mother; and finally, through somewhat murky circumstances, finding himself banished to Germany, to serve in the US Army.

Upon his return, part of Colonel Tom Parker's masterplan was to transform "Elvis the rebel" into "Elvis the family entertainer." It is in this period of 1960s Hollywood movies that Elvis lost connection with his greatest and singular power: his almost superhuman ability to connect with audiences, to excite them, to understand them, to move them. Not with voice, but with body and soul. Suddenly, as the world changed with the arrival of the Beatles, the Vietnam war, the civil rights movement, and heightened political division in America, Elvis was no longer at the center of cultural relevance for the first time in his career. At the precise moment when it seemed to the Colonel that the best way to monetize Elvis was to have him hang up the leather jacket and take up the mantle of a fireside, Bing Crosby–like Christmas special, Elvis met Steve Binder. It left him with a choice.

Many shenanigans, high jinks, and unbelievable twists and turns ensued, but what is indisputable and captured in this book through the eyes of the show's radical young director is the classic backstage story of an artist reconnecting with his roots and defying expectations. Steve Binder encouraged Elvis to reach back into his past, to play his early hits, and he helped Elvis find the strength to defy the Colonel with his creative choices, and refuse to put commercial considerations above the music he cared about singing as he dared to connect with a live audience once again.

The special featured several forms unheard of at that time, including an unplugged, in-the-round performance. Rather than end the show with a Christmas song, Binder created a powerful ballad in response to the tragic assassination of Robert F. Kennedy. An anthem, sung with gut-wrenching sincerity, beamed out through millions of televisions in one of the most divisive years in American history. Elvis, in his white suit, singing "If I Can Dream" was surely the moment when Elvis began to realize that he and his gift could not only be relevant again, but that they were needed.

Baz Luhrmann

Who would have thought that the 1968 Elvis NBC special would be as celebrated today as it was when Elvis Aaron Presley made his historic comeback fifty years ago?

Yes, it's been five decades since I directed and produced what half a century later would still be considered a pivotal moment in television and music history.

My early experience of Elvis was that of me sitting in front of our family television set watching his first *Ed Sullivan Show* appearance. Seeing his audience, consisting of mostly young girls, hysterically screaming, shouting, and almost drowning out his vocal performance was amusing and definitely exciting. In 1963, Elvis's career had stagnated when the British invasion came to America. A sea of fresh, young artists like the Beatles and the Rolling Stones were launching their careers in America. As his successful film career was coming to an end, even Elvis wondered if his time as a rock 'n' roll superstar was finished.

Colonel Tom Parker, Elvis's infamous personal manager, was desperate to reinvigorate Elvis's career and make him relevant again. Nearly five years before the Elvis special aired, the Beatles proved how powerful the television medium could be. Their own appearance on the Sullivan show was a large part of their stratospheric success.

None of my staff, including me, ever imagined we were making history by breaking the mold in so many ways. Never before had one artist, without any guest stars, dominated the television screen for the entire hour of primetime television. Today, television audiences are splintered across many cable and network channels, so it might be hard to believe that more than 40 percent of American households tuned into the Elvis special to see what all the fuss was about. We just knew it was an opportunity to do something completely different from the norm. We were working with an artist who was rediscovering himself and loving the hell out of it!

Clad in black leather, a well-tanned and toned Elvis (thanks to a Hawaiian holiday before we began rehearsals) owned the moment. He also owned it in a white suit and gold lamé jacket. Elvis was collaborative and embraced a real sense of joy in the process of working with all of my extremely talented crew and staff members, who you'll enjoy meeting in this book. We saw his confidence restored as he returned to his roots. We saw him connect with his audience and find a new legion of fans, too. We saw Elvis make magic. It was fantastic to witness this historic event in person.

The entire process wasn't without a few hiccups. I have documented the behind-the-scenes story as best I could. I also share some of the spine-tingling moments that were witnessed while in production. To this day in 2018, it is still a relevant story. The special stands firmly as a great moment in TV history. I am humbled and honored to be a part of it.

Today's staging of televised live event musicals is the closest thing current audiences come to experiencing the electricity of what was possible fifty years ago. At the time, television was unprepared for the unleashing of Elvis to come back to his musical roots when he would later and forever firmly establish his title as the King of Rock 'n' Roll. I hope you enjoy reading my book as much as I enjoyed writing it.

Steve Binder / Director-Producer
Oxnard, California
August 2018

SINGER* PRESENTS ...

NBC TV / DECEMBER 3 / 9 PM (EST)

ACKNOWLEDGEMENTS

I'd like to acknowledge my talented television family who participated in the making of *ELVIS*. Each one of them contributed greatly to its success.

This special, part of a trilogy of shows that we worked on together, beginning with *Hallelujah Leslie* starring Leslie Uggams, continuing with *Petula* starring Petula Clark with guest star Harry Belafonte, and culminating with *ELVIS*. These amazing and talented people behind the scenes were: executive producer Bob Finkel; my talented partner at the time and record producer, Bones Howe; writers Allan Blye and Chris Bearde; music director and arranger Billy Goldenberg; choral director and composer of the song, "If I Can Dream," Earl Brown; art director Gene MacAvoy; costume designer Bill Belew; choreographers Claude Thompson and Jaime Rogers, and production assistant Pat Rickey.

Additionally, I would like to honor Elvis's musicians Scotty Moore and DJ Fontana for participating in the acoustic portions of the show and the famous Los Angeles studio musicians, known as the original Wrecking Crew. Chris Bearde, DJ Fontana, Scotty Moore, Earl Brown, Bill Belew, and Claude Thompson have passed on, but will always be remembered for their great contributions to this now-historical event in television history.

I dedicate this book to my family who have stood by and encouraged me throughout my life. I was blessed with a fantastic mom and dad who taught me the values of love and integrity. To my sister, Ilene, and my wife, Sharon. I couldn't have written this book without their love and support; my children from a former marriage to Judith, and our children Dana Sigoloff and Romy Harding. To my talented son-in-law, Stephen Sigoloff, and my grandkids, Alex and Erin Sigoloff and Kendall and Kaila Harding; my nephews Michael and Jeff Ball and Jeff's wife, Stephanie, and their children Lucien and Shawn; and to my extended family, Nathan and Christine Weber; our grandkids Natalie and Kayla Weber, and Mike Clark, Mercury and baby Zela, and Alex and Daylen Clark. And finally, Jeff Abraham, my friend and Elvis devotee. They all constantly remind and inspire me to set a good example for them as a husband, father, grandfather, and friend.

I will forever be grateful to them all.

MEMORIES PRESSED BETWEEN THE PAGES OF MY MIND
MEMORIES SWEETENED THROUGH THE AGES JUST LIKE WINE

Two lines from the song lyric "Memories," written by Billy Strange and Mac Davis, and sung for the first time by Elvis Presley on his 1968 NBC television special.

I would like to hold out my arms, my heart, and lifetime friendship to Spencer Proffer. I cannot thank him enough for his passion, vision, and longtime support of my work. In putting this book together, Spencer made this dream of mine come true well beyond my expectations.

To my graphic designer, the ever-so-talented Hugh Syme, I thank him for his genius and dedication to making this book a true passion project for him as well as for me.

My thanks to Matt Abruzzo and Marc Rosen (ABG); Jack Soden, Gary Hahn and Laurie Williams (Graceland); Judith A. Proffer; Daren Miller, Bethany Claypool, Lindsay Tarnowski, Kate Kelly, Ray Nutt, Gordon Synn, Tommy Nast, Melanie Poehner, and Jessica Nelson (Fathom Events); Dan Diamond and Shelly Maxwell (Kaos Connect); Baz Luhrmann, Sam Bromell; Dave Harding, John Scheinfeld, Morgan S. Proffer (Sorski Media), Sterling Proffer; Jay Jarvis, Joey Porterfield, and Kim McMasters (Music Today); Sarah Casey (Logovision); David Humphrey, Peter Levshin (ICLA); John Kavanaugh (103.2 Dublin City FM); Jeroen Vanderschoot (Elvis Matters Fan Club, Belgium); Alanna Nash, Debra Amona, Lawrence H. Brown, Kory Grow (*Rolling Stone* magazine); and Priscilla Presley.

I'd like to add a special shout-out to all the talented cast and crew who participated in one of the greatest events in entertainment history. I have the utmost admiration for you all.

Special thanks to Joe Tunzi for his belief in this project.

Long live the King of Rock 'n' Roll.

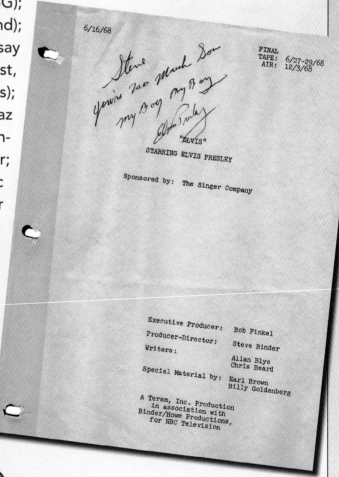

Steve Binder and Elvis on set at NBC Studios

ABOUT THE AUTHOR

Steve Binder is an EMMY and ACE award-winning producer, director, writer, educator, and Golden Globes nominee. The *Los Angeles Times* called his first feature film, *The T.A.M.I. Show*, "the greatest of all rock 'n' roll films." Steve has written, produced, and directed dozens of television specials, including multiple Diana Ross specials as well as *Petula* with British singer Petula Clark and Harry Belafonte. He has frequently been a guest speaker at the William S. Paley Media Center in Los Angeles and New York where special evenings were devoted to his work in the entertainment industry.

In 1968, he conceived, directed, and produced *ELVIS, The '68 Comeback Special. TV Guide* called this landmark event "the second greatest musical moment in television history next to the Beatles debut on the *Ed Sullivan Show*." Steve proudly served in the US Army in Europe as an announcer for the Armed Forces Radio network. He is currently an active member of the Directors and Producers Guilds of America. Binder serves as an adjunct professor at the University of Southern California.

His favorite saying is "Whatever you do in life, do it with passion."

Without a doubt, the most important show that I ever produced and directed was the 1968 NBC special titled simply *ELVIS*. I know that there are dozens of books, blogs, and movies written and made about the special. Now it's time to tell *my* story about what is considered by fans and critics alike as one of the greatest comebacks in show business history.

ELVIS AND BINDER-HOWE PRODUCTIONS

On February 1, 1968, at exactly 5:01 p.m., Priscilla Presley gave birth to daughter Lisa Marie, nine months after she and Elvis were wed. That month, I was meeting with legendary feature film producer Walter Wanger (*Gung Ho*, 1943; *I Want to Live*, 1958; *Cleopatra*, 1963) who wanted me to direct his next film. I was well into working on the script with Wanger when a call came into my office from NBC television producer Bob Finkel. Bob said he had just read about "the touch" on my Petula Clark–Harry Belafonte special earlier that same year. Even though I had shot multiple takes of their duet ("On the Path of Glory") without either of the two stars touching each other, I had refused to remove the take with "the touch" before it broadcast on national TV, despite objections from the sponsors. It was the first time in a primetime national television variety show that a white and a black performer had physical contact of that nature.

It was considered groundbreaking.

Apparently Finkel thought the controversy surrounding the special and my reputation at the time as a young rebel would make me a perfect fit for Elvis Presley. He explained to me that some time before, Tom Sarnoff, then-chairman of NBC, had run into Elvis's legendary manager Colonel Parker at a social event. The two had worked out a deal for NBC to finance Elvis's next feature film—that is, providing Elvis would commit to doing a one-hour NBC television special to be broadcast in December. Bob told me he was planning on producing and possibly directing the special himself, but was not sure it would ever really get made because Elvis was balking at doing television. He was also concerned that after meeting Elvis on several occasions, Elvis continued to politely address him as "Mr. Finkel" instead of Bob. He felt Elvis needed a director he could relate to, someone closer to his own age. Once the right director/producer was found, Bob would then take on the role of the show's executive producer. I told him that I was committed to doing a feature film. Even though it was a tempting proposition, I had to turn him down.

Fortunately my partner in Binder-Howe Productions, the respected record producer Bones Howe, overheard my conversation with Finkel and told me I'd be crazy if I turned down a chance to work with Elvis Presley. Before Bones had become a full-time record producer, he had engineered a couple of Elvis's albums and thought that Elvis and I would make a great combination. Bones convinced me that developing a feature film would be a long and slow process. Wanger might be persuaded to delay his project so I could do both—the feature *and* the television special.

I phoned Finkel back and told him that if a meeting could be arranged with Elvis and we were to hit it off, I would try my best to make the commitment. At that time in my career I was seriously considering leaving television and focusing on directing feature films. Fate stepped in and changed everything. Walter Wanger died of a heart attack and his feature film went away. I was available.

My first in-person meeting with Bob Finkel was at the Brown Derby restaurant in Hollywood. The Derby was world famous for its Cobb salad, grapefruit cake, and above all, its celebrity clientele in the 1940s and 1950s—hundreds of celebrity caricatures lined the restaurant's storied walls. When Bones and I arrived, we were greeted with a friendly smile and a solid hand-shake. Finkel was dressed casually. I immediately liked his demeanor. I'd been following Bob's career for years, along with fellow producer/director Bob Banner, who produced the Perry Como specials of the 1950s. The two of them represented the generation of respected variety producer/directors before I ever dreamed of getting into the entertainment industry.

After my lunch with Bob, I received the following letter from him on April 16:

Dear Steve:

As I told you during our last meeting, as soon as the Colonel clears the dates of the last two weeks of May and the first two weeks of June, we will be able to then sit down with Tom Sarnoff and work out our deal. I just spoke to the Colonel; and, there are certain contractual points being worked out between NBC and Elvis Presley which are holding up the clearance of these dates. But, I am being assured by all, that this will be decided very shortly. Thanks again for your interest. I am very happy at the prospect of us working together, and, I am sure it will be a gigantic and tremendously exciting project.

Cordially, Bob Finkel

Soon after, I received a call from Finkel saying he was prepared to hire me. He wanted Bones and yours truly to meet him at his NBC offices in Burbank. His office was impressive. A successful Emmy and Peabody Award-winning producer, Finkel had decorated his office walls with some of his accomplishments. Nearly fifty and in good physical shape, Finkel was upbeat and full of energy. His dark hair contrasted with his tanned skin and aviator sunglasses. After a brief conversation, we walked to the NBC stages where Finkel was producing both *The Jerry Lewis Show* and *The Beautiful Phyllis Diller Show*. After a short visit to the Jerry Lewis stage—where Jerry himself was warming up the live studio audience (pretending to urinate in a men's room while still wearing a forgotten microphone), we agreed to move forward with the Presley special. Bob told me that he would arrange a meeting with the Colonel as soon as possible. We parted with a good feeling about working together.

On May 7, Finkel forwarded all the Elvis material that Colonel Parker sent to his office on January 31, so I could prepare myself for the meeting with the Colonel and, hopefully, Elvis.

"WE COVER THE NATION"

Thomas A. Parker
Exclusive Management

P.O.
4-17

MADISON,
TENN.

January 31, 1968

Dear Mr. Finkel:

The Colonel asked us to send these along to you.

Col. Parker's Office

(Bio's, 45 records, tape LP catalogues, pix, cadillac brochure;
kept bios + 2 pix)

egance in action!

with the biggest, smoothest
oduction motor car!

r disc brakes are available on all models. You
choose an improved air conditioning system
s more air more quietly. A new padded instru
...concealed windshield wipers...and many
ificant improvements make all of Cadillac's
models the most elegant and exciting in
kury car world. For the complete "inside story" of
Cadillac for 1968, call on your authorized dealer soon.

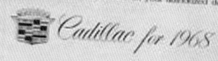

Cadillac for 1968

DAILY VARIETY DAILY

Ten Cents

Hollywood, California - 90028, Thursday, Jan. 18, 1968

Vol. 138   No. 30

PRESLEY'S 2-PLY DEAL WITH NBC

A few days later, Bob arranged a meeting with the Colonel at his MGM Studios office in Culver City. I received a strange request from Finkel to stop on the way to MGM and pick up some danish pastries for the Colonel. The meeting was scheduled very early in the morning, so I figured that we'd be joining the Colonel for breakfast with coffee and the danish I was bringing.

Colonel Parker's office was nothing like Finkel's. It didn't look like anything you'd expect to see on a famous Hollywood studio lot. It looked more like a large kitchen in a middle-class southern home. A large table sat in the room's center, surrounded by oak chairs. Sitting on high barstools in the back of the room were Tom Diskin (the Colonel's right-hand man) and Freddy Bienstock, an executive from their Hill & Range Publishing Company. They were there to greet us. Upon entering his office with Bones, I handed the Colonel the bag full of the pastries. I watched curiously as he squirreled them directly into his briefcase while motioning us to sit at the table. The entire time we talked, there was no mention of coffee or the pastries.

For the next thirty minutes, the Colonel did all the talking—starting with a dancing chicken story. Parker had worked in a carnival and his "act" was getting people to buy tickets to see his chickens. He told us that he had seven live chickens and a hot plate covered with straw. When he plugged the electrical cord into the socket (with "Turkey In The Straw" blasting on the speakers) the birds would start jumping up and down to avoid the extreme heat. I thought it was sadistic, barbaric . . . and definitely not funny.

Next, the Colonel showed us a copy of Presley's contract with the studio. He went on to brag that if there were to be a dispute between him and MGM, it would take less than an hour to pack up and be off their lot. He claimed that he had a Bekins moving van parked on the lot, ready to go, if necessary (not true). He bragged about his one page standard contract that he had with all the film studios whenever Elvis made a movie. The contract stipulated exactly how many days Elvis would be required to film and what time he would start work and what time he could leave each day. He pointed out to us that the most important clause in the contract was the one-million-dollar fee for Elvis's services. The Colonel told us that once the contract was fully executed, Elvis would do anything the studio or the producer asked of him as long as it was in the contract.

Evidently the Colonel wanted to impress us with what he considered to be his astute business sense. In my opinion, it was a terrible contract. It did not require the studios to give Elvis any ownership in his movies, nor were there any provisions for ancillary rights that would have added up to millions more. Worse yet, Elvis would be required to sing *any song* that the writer put in the script. Many of the screenwriters of his movies intentionally wrote songs for Elvis to sing in their movies, thinking only of the monies *they* would earn in songwriting royalties, even though they were not professional songwriters.

Near the end of the forty-five-minute meeting, the Colonel handed me two gifts. One was a box with Presley's face on the front cover surrounded by snow-capped mountains and bas-relief pine trees. Inside the box was an audio tape and a color brochure of Elvis holding the back of a cane chair and dressed in a red Eisenhower jacket, white shirt, and black pants with the title, "Season's Greetings from Elvis." The back of the brochure read: "The complete script for Elvis's Special Christmas Program scheduled on your station for Sunday, December 3, 1968."

The script inside the brochure, in bold red print, had the timings for all the songs and public service announcements, and was titled "Elvis's Special Christmas Program Script." It contained a breakdown of Elvis Christmas songs: "Here Comes Santa Claus," "Blue Christmas," "O Little Town of Bethlehem," "Silent Night," "I'll Be Home for Christmas," "I Believe," "If Every Day Was Like Christmas," "How Great Thou Art," and "His Hand in Mine." Buzz Benson was the announcer who read the text between each song. After "O Little Town of Bethlehem," he introduced a scripted public service announcement by actor Dale Robertson, then-star of the *Iron Horse* television show that aired on ABC Monday nights. Robertson read the short script—his plea to the listeners to contribute to Christmas Seals as "a true American holiday tradition." He never once mentioned the name Elvis. When the announcement was over, two more Elvis Christmas songs followed, promoting two different RCA Victor Elvis albums. Elvis finally spoke his one and only five-second message on the 7.5-inch reel-to-reel tape after Benson's forty-second-long introduction.

Benson's intro to Elvis included a promotion of the RCA Elvis Christmas album and the United Artists motion picture *Clambake*. It ended with "And now, *heeere's* Elvis . . ." in a true Ed McMahon flourish. Following Presley's five seconds on tape was his singing of "I'll Be Home for Christmas."

The very last minute of the tape reel read: "NOTE: This one minute to be used for a local message for a charity of your choice." Buried in the bottom of the box was a new 45-rpm record released by RCA Victor. The A side was "If Every Day Was Like Christmas" and the B side was "How Would You Like to Be" from *It Happened at the World's Fair*. That box was the Colonel's Christmas gift to an estimated four thousand local disc jockeys at radio stations across America. As the Colonel handed me the box, he told me it contained what was going to be the NBC "Elvis Christmas Special." There was no question in my mind that the Colonel meant every word of it.

The second gift was a membership card and booklet to his Snowmen's Club with the inscription:

"To Snower Steve Binder."

Under my name it read:

*There is nothing I can give you
which you have not
But there is much while I cannot
give you you can take.
— Fra. Giovanni*

It was signed simply "Potentate."

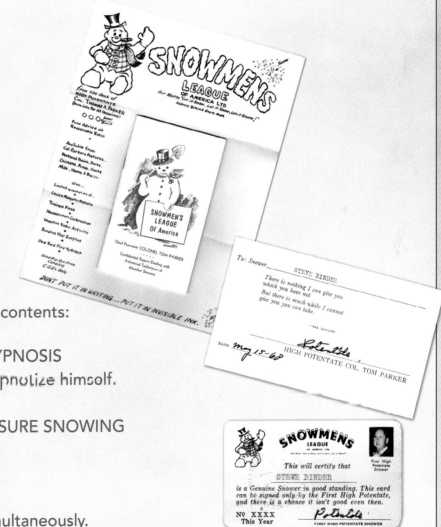

Inside the booklet was an amusing table of contents:

Chapter 1 - SNOWING AS RELATED TO HYPNOSIS
How a member snowed the hypnotist to hypnotize himself.

Chapter 2 - COUNTERACTING HIGH PRESSURE SNOWING
Melt-and-disappear technique.

Chapter 3 - DIRECTIONAL SNOWING
This deals with approach and departure simultaneously.

Chapter 4 - ADVANCED SNOWING TECHNIQUES AND WHERE IT LEADS
With sufficient training one can develop the ability to go nowhere with devastating results.

Chapter 5 - WHAT SNOWING DOES FOR YOUR INCOME
Learn how you can make your Income catch up with your outgo—frozen assets thawed and sinking funds refloated.

Chapter 6 - SNOWING AS A STATUS SYMBOL
How a member had the good fortune to be drummed out of the PTA.

Chapter 7 - SNOWING AND SOCIABILITY
It sets the member apart and sometimes can lead to exile.

The membership card held the Colonel's picture and his signature snowman cartoon on the upper portion. Below that it read: "Snowmen's League of America Ltd. Our motto Let it Snow, Let it Snow, Let it Snow! This will certify that Steve Binder is a Genuine Snower in good standing. This card can be signed only by the First High Potentate, and there is a chance it isn't good even then." The Colonel went on to explain that to be a member in the club, you had to be a great bullshitter. I accepted the cards and booklet, but hoped he realized I wasn't worthy of his "honor."

The meeting was over, we all shook hands and said our goodbyes. The Colonel promised to set up a meeting with Elvis at the Binder-Howe offices on Sunset Boulevard later that day. All the while Bones and I were there, I studied the Colonel studying me. It was a pleasant enough meeting—like the start of a poker game where everybody at the card table is sizing up the opposition before the high-stakes game begins.

Some Elvis insiders already knew that the Colonel, when making the deal with NBC, insisted that the television special be a Christmas show with Elvis merely saying "Hello . . . Merry Christmas . . . and Goodnight" in between singing twenty-six Christmas songs. NBC didn't care what the show was as long as they got Elvis on the air and found a sponsor to pick up the tab for the show.

ELVIS PRESLEY
SPECIAL CHRISTMAS PROGRAM

SEQUENCE	
	(5 SECONDS)
	(27 SECONDS)
	(2 SECONDS)
INTRO: "HERE COMES SANTA CLAUS"	(23 SECONDS)
ANNOUNCER	(2 MIN. 5 SEC.)
"HERE COMES SANTA CLAUS"	(13 SECONDS)
ANNOUNCER	(2 MIN. 34 SEC.)
"BLUE CHRISTMAS"	(9 SECONDS)
ANNOUNCER	(1 MIN. 13 SEC.)
"O LITTLE TOWN OF BETHLEHEM"	(12 SECONDS)
ANNOUNCER	(2 MIN. 23 SEC.)
MR. ROBERTSON	(2 MIN. 39 SEC.)
ANNOUNCER	(1 MIN. 39 SEC.)
"SILENT NIGHT"	(20 SECONDS)
"I'LL BE HOME FOR CHRISTMAS"	(2 MIN. 4 SEC.)
ANNOUNCER	(20 SECONDS)
"I BELIEVE"	(2 MIN. 51 SEC.)
ANNOUNCER	(30 SECONDS)
"IF EVERY DAY WAS LIKE CHRISTMAS"	(16 SECONDS)
ANNOUNCER	(2 MIN. 58 SEC.)
"HOW GREAT THOU ART"	(3 SECONDS)
ANNOUNCER	(19 SECONDS)
"HIS HAND IN MINE"	(17 SECONDS)
BACKGROUND MUSIC "I'LL BE HOME FOR CHRISTMAS"	(40 SECONDS)
ANNOUNCER	
(PICTURE RELEASE)	(5 SECONDS)
ELVIS: SPECIAL ELVIS MESSAGE	(1 MIN. 34 SEC.)
"I'LL BE HOME FOR CHRISTMAS"	(7 SECONDS)
ANNOUNCER	(1 MINUTE)
LOCAL MESSAGE	

A complete script for Elvis' Special Christmas Program scheduled on your station for Sunday, December 3, 1967 in enclosed

SEASON'S GREETINGS FROM ELVIS

The complete script for Elvis' Special Christmas Program scheduled on your station for Sunday, December 3, 1967.

Their sales department already had a sponsor relationship with Farlan Myers at J. Walter Thompson Advertising Company, who represented Singer Sewing Machines. As a favor to Farlan and his advertising agency, NBC practically gave them the Elvis special as part of a package deal. Singer also bought two more specials that year to air on NBC, featuring Don Ho from Hawaii and pianist Liberace. Kentucky Fried Chicken and Mrs. Paul's Fishsticks tried desperately to sponsor the Elvis show and probably would have doubled or tripled the license fee that Singer actually paid for it.

The first meeting with Elvis took place at the Binder-Howe offices right on the Sunset Strip at 8833 Sunset Boulevard, Suite 410, on Friday, May 10. Elvis, looking amazing, arrived at the prearranged time of 4:00 p.m. accompanied by his road manager, Joe Esposito; Charlie Hodge, an army buddy he met while stationed in Germany; Lamar Fike, a member of Elvis's inner circle who had a distinguished career in the music business; and Alan Fortas, whose uncle Abe Fortas was a Supreme Court justice. The entourage sat in our reception area while Elvis, Bones, and I went behind closed doors. Elvis immediately referred to me by my first name. When Finkel heard about that later, he knew he had made the right decision.

My first impression of Elvis was he was physically perfect. His facial features were flawless, reminding me of the sculptured Statue of Liberty face. Usually, most stars have a favorite side of their face that they insist the director favor while being photographed. Not Elvis. He was perfect from any angle.

We chatted in my office for about an hour. Elvis asked me where I thought his career was at now, and I told him jokingly, "in the toilet." I think he immediately respected my blunt honesty and said to me, "Finally, somebody is speaking the truth to me." He told me about his reluctance to do a television special because he hadn't appeared in front of a live audience for years, and he wasn't sure they'd even accept him now, especially since the Beatles were at the pinnacle of their success in America. I told him that if we did work together there would be a big risk involved. If the special tanked, he would still be remembered as an old rock 'n' roll and movie star of the 1950s and early 1960s who had a fantastic career and a personal manager, but essentially his career would be over. On the other hand, if the special were a success, he'd instantly be able to reestablish himself as the King of Rock 'n' Roll.

I told Elvis that if we did this special right, it wasn't going to be just a lot of songs strung together with pretty scenery and colorful costumes, but a subliminal tale of his personal life's journey. At the end of the day, viewers would really feel they knew him as a compassionate and loving person as well as a great singer and entertainer.

"I love it," he said. "Let's do it." So, we did.

I asked Elvis if Bones and Jimmy Webb had offered the song "MacArthur Park" to him instead of Richard Harris, would he have recorded it? Without hesitation, he answered a definitive "Yes." At the time we were having this conversation, Bones was exclusively producing hit records for the 5th Dimension and the Association. Bones commissioned Jimmy Webb to write a new song for the upcoming Association album, entitled "Birthday." There was great anticipation for their new album after their first album had hit songs on it like "Windy," "Cherish," and "Never My Love." The Association made a regrettable mistake by turning down Jimmy's new song, "MacArthur Park," and so Jimmy recorded the song with actor Richard Harris in England.

When I taped the acoustic/improvisation segment for the special months later, that conversation must have still been on Elvis's mind, because he sang a few lines from the song several times during the segment. I remember asking Elvis what he thought of today's music and the different rock bands, and he said he liked some of the music and thought some of the new rock bands were great, specifically mentioning the Beatles. He went on talking unhappily about his past television experiences and how he felt they were out of his comfort zone because the only turf he felt comfortable on was in a recording studio. I knew what he was talking about, because I felt that he was treated by many in show business as a novelty act instead of a serious artist.

Steve Allen had him dress in a tuxedo with a live basset hound in front of him while he sang "Hound Dog." Milton Berle made fun of him on his slapstick variety show. After his third appearance on the *Ed Sullivan Show*, his popularity with his youth audience accelerated. CBS feared that his gyrations would somehow corrupt the youth of America, so they instructed the director to only shoot Elvis from the waist up. The next day he was the major topic of conversation in every household and at every office water cooler across America.

After listening to Elvis's fears about television, I told him he could focus on making a new album while I put pictures to his music. I told Elvis we would approach his special like a tailor making a suit for a special customer. Because it was custom-made, it wouldn't fit any other artist. If the special we created for Elvis didn't feel right to him, then we'd throw out the entire concept. We wrapped up our first meeting with him telling me that he was on his way to Hawaii to get some rest and relaxation and would be back in a few weeks. I told him that while he was in Hawaii, we'd kick around a few ideas and meet again as soon as he returned to the mainland. We would then see if what we came up with was working. If he liked where we were going, we'd begin produc-tion soon after he returned; if not, we could say it was nice meeting each other and move on.

Before he left, I asked him if there was anyone in his world he wanted to have on my staff. At first he replied "No," but after thinking about it, he asked me to include guitarist and arranger Billy Strange. I had never worked with Strange, but I said that I would have no problem hiring him even though I really wanted Billy Goldenberg for that job. Goldenberg was my musical director and arranger on both my two previous specials, *Hallelujah Leslie* (Leslie Uggums, ABC) and *Petula* (Petula Clark and Harry Belafonte, NBC). I met Billy earlier in 1965 when I directed *Hullabaloo* for NBC and Billy was our dance arranger under Peter Matz (music arranger and producer of early Barbra Streisand TV specials).

Stage 4 Rehearsal

6/26/68

2ND REVISED RUNDOWN   "ELVIS"   TAPE: 6/27-29/68
                STARRING ELVIS PRESLEY   AIR: 12/3/68

1. Disclaimer   (1)

2. Peacock   (2)

3. "GUITAR MAN" Opening   (3)
    Elvis, 89 Boys

4. Opening Commercial   (8)
    Billboard

5.   FIRST COMMERCIAL   (9)

6. Arena Segment
    "LITTLE LESS   (10)
    CONVERSATION"

7. Arena Talk   (14)
    Elvis

8. Arena
    Elvis
    a. "HEARTBREAK HOTEL" (15)
    b. "HOUND DOG"   (17)

    c. "ALL SHOOK UP"   (19)

    d. "FALLING IN LOVE   (22)
        WITH YOU"
    e. "JAILHOUSE ROCK" (24)

    f. "DON'T BE CRUEL" (27)

    g. "BLUE SUEDE SHOES" (29)

    h. "LOVE ME TENDER" (33)

9.   SECOND COMMERCIAL (38)

10. Informal Segment
    a. Talk & Songs   (39)
    b. "MEMORIES"   (46)

11.   THIRD COMMERCIAL   (48)

12. Gospel Medley   (49)
    Elvis, Blossoms, Dancers

REVISED RUNDOWN - "ELVIS"   2.

13.   FOURTH COMMERCIAL (61)

14. "GUITAR MAN" Segment
    a. Road One   (62)
        Elvis
    b. Alley Scene   (63)
        Elvis, Men
    c. "LET YOURSELF GO" (65)
        Elvis, Girls
    d. Road Two   (70)
        Elvis
    e. Amusement Pier   (72)
        Elvis, Dancers, Bits
    f. Road Three   (79)
        Elvis
    g. Club   (81)
        Elvis, Dancers, Bits

15.   FIFTH COMMERCIAL   (86)

16. "IF I CAN DREAM"   (87)
    Elvis

17. Goodnights   (90)
    Elvis

18. Commercial Billboard (91)

19. Closing Credits   (92)
    Elvis

20. NBC Production Tag   (92)

Revised show rundown

As soon as Elvis left our offi ces, I started to assemble my think-tank family to develop a concept for our next meeting with him. Ann McClelland, who was Bones's secretary before we formed our partnership, was assigned to take notes during these think-tank meetings. In these meetings we were all equals, with no pecking order based on titles or salaries. We simply met, pitched, and embellished ideas equally. To this day, I love working that way—surrounded by talented individuals speaking their minds freely.

Rather than describe those beginning Elvis days in my own words, I present the original unedited McClelland notes taken May 14–15 and 20–21 as we began our discussions with Allan Blye, Chris Bearde, Earl Brown, Bill Belew, Gene McAvoy, Claude Thompson, Jaime Rogers, Bones, and me as to what the special should look like when Elvis returned from his vacation.

MAY 14–15 PRESLEY MEETINGS AT BINDER-HOWE

Pre-production with staff to begin immediately: Meetings with Elvis to begin on June 3rd. He will be available fi ve days a week after 1:00 pm. Aim for start of pre-record on June 15th at Recording Studios. Taping last week of June, two to four days.

Karate dance by Jaime Rogers where Presley isn't directly involved. May use up to four different choreographers in the special for different feelings in each segment.

Wardrobe: Bill Belew should submit several sketches to Presley of different types of clothes.

Musical material. One Christmas song, one sacred song, four-to-six new songs, remaining to be pop, rhythm & blues, country and western, gospel, etc. Some songs from Presley's movies cannot be used. Pre-record everything that really needs an Elvis sound and anything that can't be done as well at NBC. Everything that is pre-recorded will be done as though a commercial recording session.

Have an original theme written for the show to use with titles at beginning and end. Use news films and still photos as a montage of Presley's history over the theme and titles. First nine or ten-minutes a block buster performance of only Elvis. One idea is to begin with a moving gospel-rock segment. It would be a challenge to try to top it with the rest of the show. Different segments could be broken down into R&B, C&W, gospel, pop, talking, love, sports with music, etc.

Don't dwell on the past. The excitement is what is happening now. Elvis would like to say what he feels about the music of today and the future. Blend between songs with some dialogue. He needs an intimate or segment where the audience sees that he is a real person that is warm and sincere. Idea of an interview between Elvis and Leonard Bernstein.

If show is broken into segments of different types of music, each segment could contain songs from Presley's start and progress into today and songs of the future in that particular field (i.e., R&B, C&W, etc.) Bring nostalgia, freshness and a new look in each segment.

Open another segment or two that goes beyond music. Things Presley is interested in that could be related to music and segments; automobiles, motorcycles, karate, football, horses, possible correlation between Presley and electricity.

Our creative meetings continued while Elvis vacationed in Hawaii:

MAY 20 "JUST ELVIS" MEETING AT BINDER-HOWE

Possible openings: credits with "Guitar Man" as theme. Start with soft ballad with Presley on a bare stage with stool and guitar as visible props. Begin with overture of Presley's hits with only three or four lines of each. Start with Presley singing some strong material.

Build the show keeping in mind the idea of a nightclub act where Presley performs and also communicates in some way with his studio and television audience.

Possibly three choreographers, one for spiritual segment, one for rock and roll and one for karate dance number. Dancers should be auditioned soon.

Spiritual segment: Rocking Negro gospel feeling. Use of dancers. Should be strong visual segment, universal religious feeling. Begin with a good solid beat that continually builds.

Country and Western Segment: Should have a good graphic look. Futuristic barn maybe with dancers as extras sitting on rafters. Western clothes with style. Might be workable as concert segment.

Rock and roll segment: Use of dancers. Audience in-the-round.

Find a situation where Presley can meet with some of the people that influenced him, such as Johnny Cash, Jerry Lee Lewis, etc. Could be worked into C & W segment.

Every other segment might be in a theater-in-the-round with the last song of each segment leading into the next segment, which is in a different setting.

POSSIBLE SONGS FOR THE SHOW

1. Hound Dog
2. Don't Be Cruel
3. Love Me Tender
4. I'm All Shook Up
5. Jailhouse Rock
6. Too Much
7. Loving You
8. Teddy Bear
9. Are You Lonesome Tonight
10. Heartbreak Hotel
11. One Night
12. Return to Sender
13. A Little Less Conversation
14. Guitar Man
15. U.S. Male
16. Blue Suede Shoes
17. Fever
18. Can't Help Falling in Love
19. Little Sister
20. I'll Be Home for Christmas
21. I Believe
22. How Great Thou Art
23. Love Me

Sent to Norman Morrell 4/5/68

EXPENSES INCURRED BY BINDER/HOWE PRODUCTIONS RELATING TO
THE ELVIS PRESLEY SPECIAL FROM MAY 10 - JUNE 6, 1968:

MAY 10   SUPPLIES FOR MEETING WITH ELVIS
          PRESLEY & AIDES: SOFT DRINKS,
          CUPS, NAPKINS, CIGARS, POTATO
          CHIPS .... $ 4.36

MAY 13   SUPPLIES FOR MEETING WITH WRITERS,
          EXEC PRODUCER & PRODUCTION STAFF:
          COFFEE, CREAM, SUGAR, SPOONS ... $ 2.38

MAY 15   SUPPLIES FOR MEETING WITH
          WRITERS: SOFT DRINKS .... $ 1.04

MAY 16   SUPPLIES FOR MEETING WITH WRITERS
          & PRODUCTION STAFF: CRACKERS,
          CHEESE, NAPKINS, APPLE CIDER,
          CANDY .... $ 3.88

MAY 20   SUPPLIES FOR MEETING WITH WRITERS,
          EXEC PRODUCER, PRODUCTION STAFF:
          SOFT DRINKS, COFFEE, SUGAR, COCOA,
          SPOONS .... $ 3.61

MAY 21   SUPPLIES FOR MEETING WITH WRITERS
          & PRODUCTION STAFF: SOFT DRINKS,
          CRACKERS, CHEESE, CANDY, YOGURT,
          CUPS .... $ 5.26

MAY 24   SUPPLIES FOR MEETING WITH WRITERS:
          SOFT DRINKS .... $ 1.22

MAY 30   LUNCHES DURING MEETING FOR PRODUCER,
          P.A., ART DIRECTOR, PRODUCTION
          SECRETARY $11.49

MAY 21 "JUST ELVIS" MEETING NOTES AT BINDER-HOWE

The title for the special would be "JUST ELVIS"

Billboards: Singer titles come in cold off of the NBC logo with their billboard (i.e., "The following program "JUST ELVIS" is brought to you by Singer") then go straight into cold opening.

Cold Opening: *"Guitar Man" as theme. Fill the studio with one hundred–two hundred guys dressed in black, looking like Elvis. Use mirrors. Elvis, in the midst of this black carpet of guys, dressed in white, all with guitars. The guys are in frozen position when Presley is shown, then they move with him about every eight bars of music. The set is black, white and red with diagonal platforms or bridges going in different directions. Following "Guitar Man" is an original composition with Presley moving (using edit-tick,) then freeze picture, "Just Elvis" and fade to black.*

Commercial

(Segment ideas - not necessarily in show sequence)
Concert Segment: Open tight on Presley singing a ballad such as "Love Me Tender." Tape that performance twice. Once with audience (five hundred girls) and once without and cut in audience take at the end of the song nothing new or unusual. Let him move and groove with medleys of his hits interspersed with dialogue. Theater-in-the-round. A simple set, different than used in the opening. Presley should be alone with only a minimum of props.

Commercial

Mean and Evil segment: Use songs like "Trouble" from King Creole. Incorporate Karate dance. Work out a simple story line that would run through the segment. An overall "Slaughter on Tenth Avenue" feeling. Production segment with strong musical feeling and well choreographed.

Commercial

Sentimental and Spiritual segment: Possibly incorporate one Christmas song and love songs that could lead into spiritual. Dramatic, moving, choreographed, dialogue. Spiritual universal religious feeling. Rocking Negro gospel feeling. Solid beat that continually builds. Hand clapping, foot stomping. Baptist feel. Strong visual segment with swampland or "Porgy & Bess" type sets. Possibly tape this entire segment three-days in succession with different audiences (along with any other live segments) and edit best sections.

Commercial

Misc. segments with country and western, rock-a-billy, rhythm and blues, rock & roll. We will have up to 6-new songs to use, depending on what is needed.

When Elvis returned from his vacation in Hawaii he was tan and looked completely rested. We sat in my office once again and before we began, I asked him if we should wait for the Colonel to show up before talking about the show. Elvis explained that it was strictly a business arrangement, and the Colonel seldom accompanied him anywhere unless the press was present. The Colonel verified this later by telling me that he prided himself for never having spent a social evening with Elvis or even setting foot in Elvis's home for a meal.

Before Allan and Chris read Elvis the outline for the special, I reiterated to Elvis that I had no intention of doing a Christmas special. I said to him once again, "leave those to Andy Williams or Perry Como." That was my signal for Allan and Chris to begin pitching the outline they had written for the special. Both of them, especially Chris, have tremendous personalities and practically performed the show for him. I could tell by observing Elvis's facial and body reaction that he was eating it up and loved every word they were saying. In fact, when they concluded their last word, Elvis was so enthusiastic that it made me a little nervous that he didn't contest or want us to change anything.

On May 15, I sent a letter to Norman Morrel, who worked for Bob Finkel and was handling the budget for the special, asking for the following people and their fees to be confirmed: special lyrics/vocal arrangements, Earl Brown for $2,750; set designer, Gene McAvoy for $5,000; and costumes, Bill Belew for $2,500. All a far cry from today's salaries.

With everyone on board, it was time for Binder-Howe to close our deal with NBC. The entire production was owned by NBC and Finkel's company Teram, Inc., which had an exclusive contract with the network to produce shows for them. Both NBC and Teram were signatories of the Directors Guild of America, of which I am a long-standing member. Our contract was with Teram, representing both Elvis and Binder-Howe Productions. The William Morris Agency's legal department prepared the contract. According to a June 13 William Morris Agency memo from agent Howard West to David Freedman at NBC, Binder-Howe would be responsible for the writers, choral director, choreographers, and musical conductor and arranger. Teram would be responsible for the rest of the elements.

The contract required a $32,000 one-time payment to me for producing and directing a one-hour television special that included the first two reruns of the special. There is no mention of a salary for Bones's services as the show's music producer (though Bones and I were 50-50 partners on everything we did). On the third and fourth rerun, I was to be paid $3,500 each. Since video-casettes and DVDs were not part of the public marketplace in 1968, there were no provisions in the contract to cover revenues generated by such sales and there was no mention of a soundtrack album. Over the years since *ELVIS* fi rst aired on NBC, the Elvis Presley Estate, NBC, RCA, and various companies involved in distribution of the show have earned millions of dollars from it, as well as recordings of the multiplatinum soundtrack, clips, and commercials.

"JUST ELVIS"   5/27/68

RUNDOWN   TAPE 6/26/68-6/29/68
                                           AIR 12/3/68
_____

1. Disclaimer

2. NBC Peacock

3. Commercial Billboard ????

4. ~~Sing~~ Cold Opening

    a. Elvis talks about his special

    b. Elvis Impersonators - Japanese, German, African, etc.

    c. "GUITAR MAN" Opening - Elvis, One Hundred Men (all looking
                                    like Elvis)

5.   FIRST COMMERCIAL

6. a. Orchestra Tuning Up - Elvis Enters - Applause
    Walks to gigantic symphony orchestra setting. He
  ~~adt he~~ bows to conductor, to orchestra.

    b. Eight Minute Symphonic Bit - all his old hits,
       mixing modern and symphonic sounds, using
       giant chorus and full orchestra with small group
       sounds.

       Songs to choose from: "HOUND DOG," "BLUE SUEDE SHOES",
       "HEARTBREAK HOTEL", "ALL SHOOK UP", "DON'T BE ~~KK~~ CRUEL",
       "TEDDY BEAR", "WHERE MY RING", "JAILHOUSE ROCK".

7.   SECOND COMMERCIAL

8. a. Elvis in quiet talk bit. Shows pictures of his
      various haircuts, suits, etc. He shows some of
      his more ~~pr~~ peculiar momentos.

    b. Elvis sings sentimental country song.
      Sings: ~~x~~ "COTTON CANDYLAND", "HOW WOULD YOU BE"
  ~~xx~~ c. Finishes big new thing musically (with modern musicians)

9.   THIRD COMMERCIAL

10. Gospel Segment

11.   FOURTH COMMERCIAL

12. The ~~XXX~~ "MEAN CHUNK"

    Use "GUITAR MAN" as the theme for segment

    Have him continually walking through tape cuts.
             (MORE)

12. The "MEAN CHUBB" - (Cont'd)

Songs to fit in: "LET YOURSELF GO", "TROUBLE", "LIL' SISTER",
"LONG LONELY ROAD", "BIG BOSS MAN", "WHEELS ON MY FEET",
"SANTA'S BACK IN TOWN"

13.   FIFTH COMMERCIAL

14.   a. Christmas Song

      b. Elvis Talks

15. Show Closing (not necessarily in this order)

      a. Commercial Billboard

      b. Crawl

      c. NBC Film

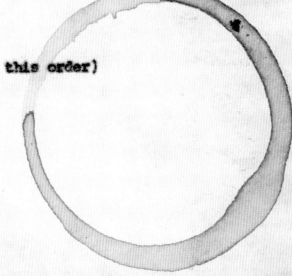

The songs listed above as "Long Lonely Road," "Wheels on My Feet," and "Santa's Back in Town"
are actually titled: "Long Lonely Highway," "Wheels on My Heels," and "Santa Claus Is Back in Town."

While my contract with NBC and Teram might seem difficult for a non-lawyer to interpret from a legal viewpoint, back in 1968, Bones and I tried very hard to protect our interests and control some of the profits for our creative work. Before we partnered up, Bones was producing records for the very successful groups the 5th Dimension and the Association. Both recording acts were at the peak of their careers and selling hundreds of thousands of copies of their albums and singles. Their records were bringing Bones a small but fair percentage of their earnings in the form of royalty payments.

Since we were the only ones producing the soundtrack to the TV special *ELVIS*, we thought the same rules should apply if the soundtrack was ever released as a recording. I phoned Fred Apollo, our agent at the William Morris Agency and explained our position to him. He understood and agreed with our position and said he would relay my message to Finkel and Colonel Parker. At the same time, he reminded me that Elvis and the Colonel were also William Morris clients and carried a lot more clout at the agency than Binder-Howe did. As soon as I hung up the phone, he called me back to say I had opened up a hornet's nest and the Colonel wanted both Bones and me off the project immediately. I held fast and maintained that our demand was 100 percent justified. The Colonel was furious and phoned me personally to tell me in no uncertain terms that "Nobody produces Elvis Presley records but Elvis himself!" and hung up on me. It was a well-known fact, but not publicized in the business, that if you were a songwriter and wanted Elvis to record one of your songs, you had to turn over 100 percent of your publishing rights to his publishing company. Bones and I stuck to our guns and didn't back off.

The solution they all came up with was that nothing in our contract would mention anything about a soundtrack album or single record. Later that day, the Colonel phoned me again—this time without the angry voice. He personally gave me his word that there would definitely be no RCA song or soundtrack album released from the television special, so we had nothing to worry about and could begin production immediately. I took the Colonel at his word. Not long after, Fred Apollo phoned me to verify that it was all taken care of and we could start back to work. He told me that there would be nothing to worry about. We should sign the contract and proceed immediately. Here's the kicker: I later learned something important from a close friend of mine who was privy to what was going on at RCA and William Morris at the time.

Even before the Colonel phoned to tell me there would be no soundtrack album, he had already made a deal with NBC and RCA calling for NBC to turn over the audiotapes from the special to RCA without charge. This was a deal that amounted to millions of dollars in music profits for Elvis and the Colonel. Elvis essentially got a free album out of the budget of the television special.

After I delivered the one-hour special to NBC, the Colonel mailed a mere $1,500 check along with an agreement for me to sign, waiving all my legal rights to the soundtrack. He even had the audacity to congratulate me on the release of the album. Instead of signing the agreement, I sent the unsigned check back to the Colonel with a short note telling him what he could do with his contract. To this day, neither Bones or I have received one penny from the soundtrack earnings.

Still, working with Elvis—especially on something as significant as his comeback—was a seminal life and career moment. I am ever grateful for the opportunity. It's just a shame that we weren't able to share in the riches beyond the richness of the experience.

This original bust of Elvis was made in Tijuana and given to me by the Colonel when we first met. Signed and dated.

PRE-PRODUCTION

I made the decision to start preparing the show at our offices on the Sunset Strip instead of driving all the way to NBC in Burbank. Allan Blye and Chris Bearde ran to the Wallich's Music City Records on the corner of Sunset Boulevard and Vine Street in the heart of Hollywood and bought up every single album that Elvis had ever recorded. They locked themselves in a room and told me they'd come out when they had determined the appropriate songs to use. Once that was accomplished, new arrangements for the songs had to be written in order for Elvis to start rehearsals with the lead sheets and piano parts for the rehearsal pianist. I phoned Billy Strange, who I had hired at Elvis's request, and asked him how soon he'd have the vocal and piano parts ready for Elvis to start rehearsing. Strange informed me that he was busy producing an album for Nancy Sinatra to capitalize on her hit record, "These Boots Are Made for Walking," yet assured me that it would be no problem handling both jobs. I took him at his word. I told him that I had scheduled rehearsals in a few weeks with Elvis at the Binder-Howe offices, and I would send him a copy of the schedule exactly when his services were needed.

Every day that followed our conversation, I made phone calls to Strange asking him, "Are you okay? Will you be able to meet your deadline?" Every day I would get the same answer: "Don't worry, I've got it under control." The rehearsal pianist I hired for Elvis was asking me to send him the piano arrangements as soon as they arrived so he'd be prepared when Elvis started rehearsals. The day was rapidly approaching when Elvis was to arrive and not one lead sheet or arrangement had been delivered to my office. I phoned Strange and demanded that he deliver anything he had completed so that we could start work when Elvis arrived. When I knew that the deadline was upon us, and we still had nothing from Billy Strange—no lead sheets or arrangements—I called him one last time and told him that if I came to my office the next day and there were no lead sheets or arrangements sitting on my desk, I would fire him. Strange told me that if it came to one of us being fired, he had the direct line to Elvis and I would be the one to go, then hung up on me. I immediately phoned Finkel and told him what was going on, that I was going to keep my word and fire Strange if I didn't receive anything from him first thing in the morning. He listened and responded with "Fire him!" So the following morning, I did just that. It was great just knowing that I had an executive producer who stood behind me and supported my decisions.

When the Colonel learned what I had done, he was furious. He told me that he doubted if Elvis would even come to work, so I phoned Elvis and explained the situation to him. His reaction was that it was no big deal. He asked who I was intending to hire to replace Billy as his music director and I told him that I was going to try to fly in Billy Goldenberg from New York, whom I totally trusted. We hung up the phone and though he had no idea who Goldenberg was, Elvis seemed perfectly satisfied and promised to show up on the first day of rehearsal.

Enter Billy Goldenberg. Billy and I first met in 1965 on the NBC *Hullabaloo* television series. Before that, Goldenberg was a kid ghostwriting for iconic Broadway composer Frank Loesser (*Guys & Dolls*, *The Most Happy Fella*) and a dance arranger for conductor/arranger Peter Matz (Marlene Dietrich, Noel Coward, and Barbra Streisand's early albums and television specials).

I wanted to hire Billy Goldenberg in the first place after our collaboration on *Hallelujah, Leslie!* and *Petula*. What I didn't count on was being turned down! When I phoned him, Billy explained that he couldn't see himself conducting "Hound Dog" or "Blue Suede Shoes" and I should get someone else who was more familiar with Elvis's music. Billy told me that he was just a kid from New York who was nourished on music from Broadway and the classics. He said how sorry he was and despite wanting to help me, he would have to pass. I wasn't about to take no for an answer. I was no longer asking. I literally begged him to take the job. I needed Billy to get on a plane to Los Angeles now. He heard the desperation in my voice. The next thing I knew, he was in my office, sitting at our upright piano as Elvis walked through the door.

Billy would turn out to be a key member of our creative family, the person mainly responsible for Elvis's newfound passion for big orchestras. From that day forward until we moved out to Burbank and NBC, Elvis and his entourage would drive into our parking garage off Sunset Boulevard at 4:00 p.m. in Elvis's Lincoln Continental with Tennessee license plates. First Elvis walked in, followed by Joe Esposito, Lamar Fike, Alan Fortas, Charlie Hodge, and on occasion, Elvis's film stand-in, Lance LeGault.

Billy and Elvis hit it off immediately. Here were this young Jewish kid from New York, a classically trained Broadway composer/conductor/arranger, with the King of Rock 'n' Roll, a southern kid born in Tupelo, Mississippi, and raised in Memphis, Tennessee, about to get together in what turned out to be one of if not *the* greatest music collaboration in music history. Who would have ever dreamed this would be possible? Billy once told me that Elvis loved to play classical music on the piano when they were alone. His favorite piece was Beethoven's "Moonlight Sonata." Billy said that if any of his guys were within listening distance, Elvis would stop playing the classics for fear they would see it as a sign of weakness.

Colonel Parker would occasionally arrive by himself and sit in our reception area while Elvis went to work with Billy, Earl, and me in our piano room. Allan and Chris had their own office next to ours and occasionally dropped in when they had a new idea or to socialize.

And as odd as this sounds, I remember seeing the Colonel at times sit in the reception area with the Elvis entourage, seemingly hypnotizing them into believing that they were farm animals. Who knows if the Colonel, who fancied himself an amateur hypnotist, was really doing it or if they were humoring him. It was a bizarre sight, nonetheless.

Soon after daily rehearsals were underway, I saw Elvis gazing out onto Sunset Boulevard through our fourth-floor window. One day I asked him what he thought might happen if he walked onto Sunset by himself. He turned to me and smiled and asked me what *I* thought would happen. I thought for a moment, then told him that I really didn't think anything would happen. "This is 1968 and kids are a lot more sophisticated these days." And we went back to rehearsing. A few days later, Elvis walked into the office and said to me, "Let's go!" I asked him, "Where to?" He said, "Down to Sunset Boulevard to test out the theory." I'm sure at the time Elvis thought he couldn't go out in public because the Colonel had likely told him he would be mobbed and possibly physically harmed by his adoring fans. Overhearing our conversation, the entourage started heading for the front door like a pack of wolves, but Elvis told them to stay put and watch us from the window.

Our building had a unique glass-enclosed elevator that looked out onto the street. Directly across the street from our office building was a topless nightclub, the Classic Cat. When Elvis and I walked out of the elevator and onto Sunset there were hardly any people on the street.

The traffic was building up on the four-lane strip in both directions with commuters and delivery trucks scurrying from or to their destinations. It became a little awkward for both of us because neither of us had a clue as to what to expect. So we started by feigning some conversation about nothing important. Just small talk. Cars were driving by, not even bothering to look at us. No horns were honking and no California girls were rolling down their windows to get a look at Elvis or scream out his name to get his attention. A couple of seedy-looking hippies almost bumped into us as they were heavily engaged in their own conversation.

After what seemed like an eternity but in reality was only a few minutes, I could tell Elvis was getting uncomfortable and restless. Absolutely nothing unusual was happening, and I sensed the window upstairs was filled with his guys making wisecracks about us down below. A few more minutes passed before Elvis decided to take charge of the situation. He started waving at the cars passing by and even shouting "hello" at some of the passengers. Still, nothing happened.

Finally, Elvis had had enough and asked me if we could go back upstairs. I was actually relieved. I assumed no one believed that it was *really* Elvis Presley standing there. Had they known it was the real Elvis, it could have been a nightmare, a huge traffic jam and a headache for all of us. But none of this happened because Hollywood was filled with guys who wanted to look like Elvis and that continues even to this day. When we went back upstairs, I sensed a different attitude in my relationship with Elvis. Moving forward, until the end of the shoot, he sought my opinion about everything. From that incident on Sunset Boulevard, Elvis had begun to *really* trust me.

NBC sent me a memo on May 14 that Studio 4 would be reserved for our show during the period of June 24–29. Rehearsal halls 3 and 4 would be reserved from June 3–23. Before production began in earnest at NBC on Monday, June 3, Elvis asked to view his turf (Studio 4) where we would be shooting the show.

Guest relations met us at the artist entrance to escort us to the stage and dressing rooms. We drove out from my office in West Hollywood to the NBC studios in Burbank, about a forty-minute drive over Laurel Canyon. When we arrived at the main gate, we were provided with a parking place reserved for us next to the artist entrance. We were to go inside the building and wait for someone to escort us to the stage. A small group of tourists were gathered inside the entrance waiting for their tour guide to escort them to the Bob Hope and Johnny Carson stages, dressing rooms, scenic and prop shops, commissary, and other typical behind-the-scenes places. We stood within a few feet of the gathering tour groups. Inside the darkened hallway, waiting patiently for our escort to arrive, Elvis was dressed casually in denim and his signature sunglasses. An elderly woman from one of the tours spotted us and made a beeline over to us. Oh oh, was the frenzy that didn't happen on Sunset Boulevard about to happen here?

The last thing I wanted was for Elvis to be bothered by a fanatical fan. Boy, was I wrong! "Excuse me, young man," she said, looking directly at Elvis, "Do you know if there are any celebrities around here today?" Elvis removed his sunglasses, smiled down at her, and said, "Sorry, ma'am, but I have no idea," and with that, put his sunglasses back on. She had no clue that she was talking with one of the biggest celebrities in the world! After apologizing for interrupting our conversation, she returned to her tour group, all oblivious to who was standing just a few feet away from them.

Our NBC guide escorted Elvis and me through the artist entrance, right next to Stages 1 and 2. Bob Hope and George Burns taped their specials on both of those stages and Johnny Carson did his nightly *Tonight Show* on Stage 1. The elephant stage doors, named for the huge doors where tall sets can be moved in and out easily, were painted with pictures of Johnny and a few of the other major stars who did their shows on those particular stages. Directly across the hall from these stages were rehearsal halls 3 and 4 where our two dance companies with choreographers Claude Thompson and Jaime Rogers would soon be rehearsing with their separate dance troupes. Down the hall and to the left were Stages 3 and 4.

I showed Elvis our rehearsal halls and Stage 4 and let him pick the dressing room that he felt he'd be most comfortable in. He chose Dean Martin's room, whose show was going on hiatus soon. Before we left NBC, Elvis seemed completely satisfied with his new turf. Then we headed back to work at the Binder-Howe offices.

On June 6, Bobby Kennedy (RFK) came to downtown Los Angeles to deliver a presidential stump speech at the Ambassador Hotel. Shortly after midnight, Kennedy was assassinated. That night, Elvis, Billy Goldenberg, Earl Brown, and I were still rehearsing the music for the special at our offices. Allan Blye and Chris Bearde were working on the script in their office next to ours. The television set was on in the office next to the piano room and we all heard a loud cacophony of noise coming from that office. We stopped rehearsing and ran to see what all the commotion was about. We, like all Americans, were stunned by what we saw on live TV. Bobby was pronounced dead a few minutes later.

The next few hours, we all talked about President John Kennedy, Dr. Martin Luther King, and now Bobby, each gunned down by an assassin's bullet. Elvis asked the sad and heavy question, "What is happening to our country?" That moment brought us closer than ever to Elvis and gave us a greater understanding of this compassionate man that we were beginning to know and love.

A few days earlier, on June 3, our dancers had started rehearsals at NBC. We continued to work with Elvis at our Binder-Howe Production offices until the choreographers were ready for him to be integrated into the full cast production numbers. We eventually moved our production people in West Hollywood to NBC Burbank so that we'd be ready to start taping the special on June 24. Our two dance companies, with choreographers Claude and Jaime, were already rehearsing with their two separate companies. About two weeks before we started taping, my assistant director Tom Foulkes and stage managers Glen Huling and Jerry Masterson would report to our rehearsal halls every morning. Goldie Hawn, one of the stars of *Laugh-In*, often dropped into rehearsals with fellow dancer Linda Shoup to visit with their friends from dance class. The staff, crew, and invited guests (such as the artists' talent managers, agents, and public relations people) would hang out in the small and narrow hallway between the two stages.

The makeup room, with enough chairs and mirrors to work on four artists at a time, was located off the hallway between the two stages and would service talent from both productions. Individual dressing rooms would line the hallway; now, the stars would be conveniently close to makeup and the stages.

Producer/director Greg Garrison and his team occupied Stage 3's control booth for the highly successful *Dean Martin Show* across the hall from our control room. I found it terribly inconvenient to have to run upstairs and downstairs whenever I wanted to talk to Elvis, so I created a mini control room on the stage where I could see the camera monitors as well as the talent simultaneously during the tapings. I have always found that talent prefers talking to a real director instead of a voice coming from a speaker.

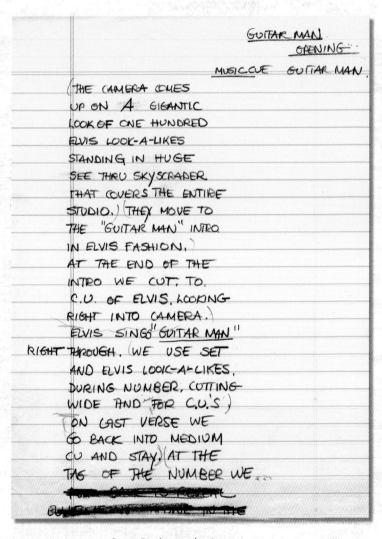

Steve Binder production notes

Steve Binder production notes

Because Elvis was so impressed with Studio 4 and its adjoining king-size star dressing room when I brought him out to NBC earlier, he made the decision to move in and live there while we were both rehearsing and taping the special. He hated the thought of having to drive every day. It really made a lot of sense to me and turned out to be a lucky decision for us all.

"When Elvis made the decision to live and sleep in his dressing room, I asked him if Priscilla and his newborn baby would be joining him. He smiled and told me he really didn't even want Priscilla to come to the studio at all while he was working. Jokingly, he said, "And besides, with all these good looking guys around . . . " Priscilla did come to see Elvis singing a medley of his classic songs in front of a live studio audience. To my knowledge, it was the only time that Priscilla came to the studio.

When Elvis finished rehearsing and taping each day, he would go to his dressing room/living quarters. After dinner he would jam with his guitar for hours at a time with anyone who happened to be hanging around. We would all sing or hum along. Elvis and the entourage would tell stories about each other and the Colonel. Sometimes we would even joke around and laugh our heads off. I don't recall Parker ever being in the room with us. Joe Esposito never left Elvis's side. I had the feeling that Joe was the Colonel's spy throughout the entire production.

In contrast to the sweet, innocent hero image that I was taping on stage, here was this raw, sexual, and sometimes even mean-spirited Elvis backstage in his converted dressing room/bedroom. I sensed right then that the King was focused on coming back to reclaim his throne in the rock 'n' roll kingdom, and that's when I got the inspiration and idea for the acoustic/improv segment.

Upon entering Elvis's dressing room with its baby grand piano in the center, you could walk through another door to a separate dressing room with a walk-in shower and bathroom. Elvis requested that we put an upright piano in the small room. Once production was underway, the improv sessions in the dressing room lasted three or four hours after a full day's work on stage. There were Dutch cigars and Pepsis everywhere. The sessions were spirited and directionless. I had to get what I was seeing every day into the show by hell or high water. But more about that later.

What became very clear to Bones and me was that Elvis had a fantastic sense of humor, which for the most part was never revealed to the general public. The day of the press conference, Tuesday, June 25 at 6:15 p.m. at NBC, we all received neck scarves with small yellow scarf holders from the Colonel as gifts from Elvis to wear when we entered the makeshift pressroom. Elvis said, "Come on, Steve, these are always fun." The Colonel positioned himself in the back of the room, standing behind the press corps. We were seated at a large table in front of the room facing the press. From left to right sat Lamar Fike, Bones, then me. Elvis was wearing a tailored silk shirt and smoking a stogie cigar. Finkel donned an all-white suit and was also smoking a stogie that Elvis handed him just as we entered the room. Joe Esposito, Charlie Hodge, and Alan Fortas stood behind us. Sitting on our table were Elvis's publicity brochures for the press to take with them when the conference ended. The front of the table was covered with black velour material so we could only be seen from our chests up. Every time a question was directed to Elvis that he thought was stupid, he would bang his leg against mine under the table signaling me that he was about to give a silly answer.

Not too long after the press conference began in earnest, Elvis answered every question, exposing to us his great sense of humor. We were all enjoying just being good listeners:

Reporter: "Elvis, why are you doing this show?"

Elvis: "We figured it was about time. Besides, I thought I'd better do it before I got too old."

Colonel Parker: (from the back of the room): "We also got a very good deal."

Reporter: "Has your audience changed much?"

Elvis: "Well, they don't move as fast as they used to."

After a few more questions and answers, the press conference itself ended abruptly. The Colonel, from the back of the room, told everyone that the press conference was over; with that, we all got up and left the room.

Left to right: Bones Howe, Steve Binder, Elvis, Bob Finkel, and Joe Esposito

"We got our money's worth out of Elvis. The special was a big event, and I thought it was terrific." —Tom Sarnoff, NBC Vice President, Production and Business Affairs

"There was a lot of creativity and inventiveness about his work, and that's why I chose Steve." —Bob Finkel, Executive Producer

A year later when Elvis opened in Las Vegas at the International Hotel, the Colonel had Elvis do another press conference very similar to the one held at NBC. It's amazing how much it echoed ours.

Reporter: Why have you waited so long to perform live again?

Elvis. I missed the live contact with an audience. It was getting harder and harder to sing in front of a camera all day (referring to his movies).

Reporter: How do you like being a father?

Elvis: I like it!

Reporter: Are you and Priscilla planning on adding to your family?

Elvis: You'll be the first to know.

Reporter: What things do you do when you are at home at Graceland?

Elvis: I ride horseback, swim, and talk with the tourists hanging out at the gate.

Reporter: How do you manage to stay so young?

Elvis: I don't know. One of these days, I'll probably fall apart. I feel I've just been lucky.

Reporter: Have you grown tired of your old movie plots?

Elvis: Yes! I want to change the type of script I've been doing.

Reporter: What kind of script do you like?

Elvis: Something with meaning. I'm going after more serious material. I couldn't dig always playing the guy who'd get into a fight, beat the guy up, and in the next shot sing to him.

Reporter: Did you like wearing leather, like the one you wore on your TV special?

Elvis: No. I hate wearing leather; they are too hot when you're working.

Reporter: Do you want to do more live shows?

Elvis: I want to. I would like to perform all over the world.

Reporter: Is it true you dye your hair?

Elvis: Sure, I have always done it for the movies.

Reporter: Why have you led such a secluded life all these years?

Elvis: It's not secluded, honey, I'm just sneaky.

Reporter: Elvis, is there anybody else you'd rather be?

Elvis: Are you kidding!

THE PRODUCTION

I was walking on the NBC lot one day when Allan Blye approached me with what I thought was a great idea. He asked if it was possible to hire one hundred Elvis look-alikes for the opening "Guitar Man" number. He explained in detail how he visualized seeing Elvis's face in a close-up and when the camera pulled back it would reveal the one hundred Elvis look-alikes playing their guitars behind him. I felt it would be a sensational opening statement, so I went to Bob Finkel, who after hearing the idea, promised that he would do his best to make it happen. He added that he wasn't very optimistic he'd get it approved by the front office. Walking away, as an after-thought, he yelled at me, "How many minutes of airtime will you be using them for?" I yelled back, "Probably no more than two minutes total." I turned around just in time to see him scratching the back of his head as he walked away. I smiled. I knew it would be a hard sell, but I could always depend on Bob Finkel to at least try. I have always felt in all of my shows that if you're lucky enough to catch one memorable moment on camera you never want to repeat it again. People will remember it forever. If you show it twice in the same show, it loses its impact. Many artists have since tried to imitate the *ELVIS* opening, so it must have been one of those moments.

When I got the word that Finkel had received approval from the front office to hire the look-alikes, my problem became where to put them. Gene McAvoy, who earlier worked as an assistant art director to Gary Smith (Smith-Hemion Productions) before Gary became a producer, came up with an idea. When they did the Judy Garland series at CBS years earlier (I vividly remembered the set), they had the signature use of her name JUDY spelled out behind her in lights thirty feet above the floor. I asked Gene to do the same for ELVIS. We had already made the decision in our think-tank sessions that the entire special would be color coordinated with only black and red scenery with the exception of wardrobe. Once this opening set was built, it was obvious that there was no room to fit all one hundred Elvis impostors in the structure, so I ended up hiring eighty-nine instead. Even that was too many. The first time we tried the shot pulling back from Elvis's close-up to reveal the set behind him spontaneous applause broke out in the booth. Elvis, dressed in black with a red bandana around his neck and the camera slowly pulling back to reveal a thirty-foot wall of Elvis look-alikes playing their guitars directly behind him sent chills down my spine.

To this day, I would love to reshoot the opening. First, I would have made sure that every "Elvis" in the scene was a musician or dancer so they would be able to follow the choreographer's instructions to move in concert with the music. Second, I would have preferred that each impostor have his own cubicle so the set appeared less congested. The truth is, once I hired the eighty-nine Elvis look-alikes, I didn't have the heart to fire even one. So I used them all.

Because I love to see dancing on television, I decided to hire thirty-six dancers, eighteen from each company. My two favorite choreographers would form two separate dance companies for the *ELVIS* special: Claude Thompson, from the earlier Petula Clark–Harry Belafonte special, and Jaime Rogers who I had met in New York while directing *Hullabaloo*.

At the time, Rogers was starring with Sammy Davis Jr. in the Broadway musical *Golden Boy*, a boxing story similar to Stallone's *Rocky*. I loved seeing Rogers dance, because he was in the original Broadway cast and feature film *West Side Story*, based on his youth in Spanish Halem. Thompson, on the other hand, was trained in ballet and jazz. The two of them made a perfect combo for what was going to be required to execute the Elvis special. Having two choreographers whose styles were so different and giving them their own choice of the many dancers we auditioned created a spirit of friendly competition that worked for the show. Thompson was responsible for the gospel segment that required his dancers to have both ballet and jazz training. Much to everyone's surprise, he cast himself in the solo that introduced the medley—surprised because Thompson was shy and introverted and the last one to put himself in the spotlight. Rogers, on the other hand, was a ball of fire with his outgoing personality and energy. Rogers was responsible for choreographing the guitar man segment, which included a very physical karate fight dance segment that showcased his skills as a soloist as well. Thinking back over the years, I think it was great that Elvis's two choreographers were Puerto Rican and African American. We live in a multicultural society and television should reflect this wherever possible. Elvis loved working with both of them equally.

During rehearsals, rumors were flying that The Beatles were constantly phoning to talk to Elvis, and he would never accept their calls. I don't know if it was true, but I do know that another entertainer from one of the other stages came over to our rehearsal hall to say "hi" to Elvis. I don't recall who it was. I just picture him walking in while the dancers were learning their steps. As he approached us, Joe Esposito stepped in before he reached Elvis and asked him what he wanted. He explained that he wanted to say "hi" to his friend Elvis. At the time, Elvis was about thirty feet away and did not look up when the conversation started. Esposito and a few others physically grabbed the "intruder" and told him to leave. He screamed to Elvis, "Do you see what your guys are doing to me?" With that he was ushered out of the rehearsal hall. I can't explain Elvis's actions that day and I was surprised that he allowed that to happen in front of all of us.

Another day in the rehearsal hall, I walked in to find a very upset Elvis sitting on a bench watching the dancers rehearsing. The minute I walked into the room, he motioned for me to sit beside him. I could tell something was on his mind. He asked me if I thought his hair was too black. At first I thought he was joking but then realized he was serious. He told me that Finkel had told him to cut back on his black hair dye. It really put Elvis into a funk. I laughed and told him to forget it, that I was sure Finkel was just having fun with him. He never brought up the subject again, but I knew how upset he was. The only other time there was a comment about his hair was during the taping of the improvisational segment. Elvis was wearing his black leather outfit under the hot lights and he was sweating profusely. An NBC executive commented to me that we might have to take this segment out of the special because his hair was messed up and not combed properly. Now I know why Elvis always used the expression, "It never ceases to amaze me, baby!"

The Colonel, frustrated and angry because his Christmas show had turned into something completely different, kept insisting that at least one holiday song be included in the special. He thought "I Believe," a hit for Frankie Laine in the 1950s, would be perfect. I never understood why he felt that "I Believe" was a Christmas song, but I knew at some point we had to come up with something to satisfy him.

I don't think the Colonel really cared whether the special was a Christmas show or not, or if there was even one Christmas song in it. All he wanted was to keep his power over Elvis in front of people who he considered "outsiders"— like me. Every decision he made that I continued to ignore, was in his mind, a direct challenge to his control over Elvis.

The Colonel loved playing one-upsmanship with Bob Finkel. They started out with playing Liar's Poker. I never played the game, but I know it had to do with the serial numbers on dollar bills and who could come up with the best poker hand. I also know that the game required a lot of bluffing. The Colonel always boasted that he was an expert at the game and the two of them played this game for hours at a time. I'm sure Bob only played to keep the Colonel out of my hair while I was busy on stage with Elvis. Apparently Finkel lost a small fortune by always letting the Colonel win.

On one occasion, Finkel received a case of Dom Pérignon as a gift from the Colonel. He told me that when they had guests over at his house the next night he opened the first bottle and instead of the expensive vintage champagne, he discovered that all of the bottles in the case were filled with Gatorade.

Another time the Colonel showed up at the studio dressed as Confederate General Robert E. Lee and presented a framed picture of himself to Bob. A few days later, Finkel rented a Napoleon-style uniform from Western Costuming, photographed himself and presented it to the Colonel.

One day while I was in the middle of taping, Elvis and I were summoned to meet the Colonel in his little broom closet of an office alongside Studio 4. He insisted upon having it, though NBC offered him a more luxurious one. Outside his door were two William Morris Agency interns assigned to him standing at attention in full Royal Guardsmen uniforms. I felt so sorry for them, and I'm sure they felt totally humiliated and embarrassed. Elvis and I entered the little office and he was sitting behind his desk, obviously in a foul mood. "Bindel"—his favorite name for me when he wasn't happy with me—"it's been called to my attention that you're not planning to have a Christmas song in the show ... Bindel, is that true?"

Two William Morris Agency interns in full Royal Guardsmen uniforms, standing at attention outside the Colonel's "broom closet" office

I replied that I really hadn't completed the entire list of songs we were using, and I didn't want to do a Christmas song that would be sung on every other Christmas show. Staring almost through me, he angrily replied, "Well, Elvis *wants* a Christmas song in the show, so we're going to do a Christmas song in the show." He turned his steel blue gaze to Elvis and said, "Isn't that right, Elvis? Tell him you want to sing a Christmas song on your show."

I looked over at Elvis standing by my side. I was hoping he would speak up, but instead he looked like a little child with his head bowed into his chin and his hands crossed in front of his private parts. He mumbled, "That's right Colonel, I do want to sing a Christmas song in the show." I remember telling the Colonel, "If that's what Elvis wants, then I'll make sure we put a Christmas song in the show." He responded, "Good, now that that's settled you boys can go back to work." We turned away from his small desk and walked out into the hallway, passing the two William Morris agents still standing at attention.

No sooner had the door closed and we were out of earshot of the two interns, Elvis jabbed me playfully in the ribs with his elbow and said, "Fuck him!" And that was that.

Following the show opening was a big production number with a huge cast, including our entire troupe of dancers, actors, extras, costumes, props, and multiple sets. Our writers Allan and Chris had woven a medley of Elvis songs from many of his old movie soundtrack albums telling a story about an innocent small-town boy who loves to play his guitar.

A young Guitar Man sets out on his coming-of-age journey to explore the world while seeking his fame and fortune. The set that Gene McAvoy created to represent the road was yellow neon tubing hung against a black velour scenic flat. The Guitar Man (Elvis) makes his first stop at an amusement park boardwalk and gets into a fight with the bully Big Boss Man, played by actor Buddy Arett, who is seen abusing his girlfriend, played by Barbara Burgess. In an act of chivalry, our Guitar Man takes on the bully. On his next stop he walks into temptation—a house of ill repute. He rejects the older, experienced prostitutes waiting for their customers and his innocent eyes go to a beautiful young girl with long blonde hair, actress Susan Hennings, who represented "innocence." Her first day at work as a prostitute and her very first encounter is with our Guitar Man.

They spotted each other across the room, moving closer and closer until finally meeting up at the exact moment the house is raided by the vice squad. The Guitar Man jumps out of the window to avoid being arrested and finds himself on the road again looking for his next adventure.

He continues his search for fame and fortune, and that's how the story goes. A framework for Elvis to sing a medley of his old songs. Every segment was shot without a live audience present and each song required costume and set changes and was being shot out of sequence. When word got out that "Binder was shooting something really risqué on Stage 4" (the prostitution scene), our show at NBC became the instant center of attention. The NBC censor assigned to the special immediately determined that the actresses playing the prostitutes were showing too much cleavage and insisted the bodices on their costumes be covered up. Our costume designer dispatched his team to find black netting and covered the exposed cleavage.

I insisted that a sponsor representative, Farlan Myers, and NBC executives Don Van Atta, Dick Loeb, and Tom Kuhn be present along with the NBC censor. They seemed to all enjoy what they saw. While this was going on, I heard a rumor that even with the girls covered up, the sponsors considered removing the entire scene from the final show. They didn't want to mention it to me for fear I would walk off the set.

Upon hearing this, I gathered them around me and told them that I wanted them all to look at the set carefully. I would rehearse the number one more time and if they had any more objections to the costumes, the set—including the brass bed in the center of the stage—now was the time to speak up. No one said a word. I then asked for their guarantee that when I finished shooting the production number it would not be removed from the final cut.

There was not one objection and that was the end of that. So I thought. Earlier Dick Loeb, an NBC executive at the time, used the word "bordello" when describing the set and mentioned it to the ad agency reps whose job was to protect their client. Singer Sewing Machine Company decided that the bordello scene might offend the little ol' ladies in the Singer Sewing Centers across the country and in spite of all their early promises and my passionate objections, it was removed from the first broadcast but reinserted on subsequent broadcasts. In some ways, that Guitar Man segment paralleled Elvis's real life.

Earlier I mentioned that I had to use one of the prebuilt sets for the improv segment because there was no time to build a new set from scratch. Gene McAvoy (our art director) told me we had exhausted our budget for the scenery, so we used an intimate boxing ring without the ropes. We featured the medley of his early hit records and called it the arena segment.

Our plan was to use our full orchestra, The Wrecking Crew, and background singers (the Blossoms) to play and sing live while Elvis sang to Billy's arrangements of his classic hits: "Heartbreak Hotel," "Blue Suede Shoes," "Jailhouse Rock," "Hound Dog," "All Shook Up," "Don't Be Cruel," "Can't Help Falling in Love," and "Love Me Tender."

Though there were times when we were forced to stop and pick up again, my intention was never to stop taping. Instead, we shot the entire segment as if it were a concert being broadcast live. I didn't even block any of my camera shots in advance. I felt strongly that I could instinctively improvise and know when to change camera angles as Elvis moved around the small boxing-ring stage.

Since there would be no post-production special effects, I did all of my own superimpositions and effects in-camera at the time we were taping. What I saw in the control room at the time of taping was exactly what viewers saw watching at home when the special was broadcast.

THE ARENA

A first in variety television was the use of a handheld camera that I had to beg NBC Sports to use for the arena and improv segments. I had seen the use of this small mobile camera by watching NBC football when they first introduced the camera mount to the public. I knew immediately that this technical invention could free up directors from the large and cumbersome studio cameras and help to capture the intimacy of a performer in handheld documentary style. I think it added great excitement to both segments.

To me, the arena segment was as important to the overall success of the production as the acoustic segment turned out to be. In that black leather suit and under the hot lights, Elvis proved once again that there were no gimmicks associated to his voice and charisma in front of a live audience. I've heard others compare his performance to watching a black panther in a cage.

They weren't far off. It was during the arena segment when I first realized that I was watching Elvis rediscover himself.

From the very beginning, I was determined to capture the *real* Elvis, not the homogenized version that was being presented whenever he appeared on his earlier television appearances or in his movies. Ordinarily, and up to this time, when singers appeared on television, they would be asked to stand on a specific mark placed on the floor directly in front of them (called a t-mark), where the lighting director would have key lights on their faces and backlights for their hair and shoulders, with one or two fill lights added.

The camera would be placed directly in front of the singer and if the director wanted him or her to move, another mark would be placed on the floor for the singer to walk to, where it would be lit and shot exactly the same way. I didn't want to ask Elvis to go to any marks on the floor, so I asked John Freschi, our lighting director, to light the entire stage so Elvis could be free to go anywhere his instincts took him. I wanted the lighting to replicate real life. As far as I was concerned, this special was not going to be traditional television. It needed to have the feel of a rock 'n' roll concert. If his hair was mussed up and he was sweating profusely—then so be it. If cameras or equipment normally hidden from the audience's view were visible in the shot . . . who would care? Well, NBC and the Singer Company evidently cared a lot. The minute they saw the raw Elvis with sweat rolling down his face from the hot lights and his leather suit, they asked me to either reshoot or take those scenes out of the special. Guess who won those battles?

Elvis was visibly nervous when we started taping. He said to the audience, "It's been a long time, baby!" . . . and you could see he meant every word. I could actually see his hand shaking as he took hold of the microphone. But once he started singing and felt the electricity in the room, he relaxed and morphed into the Elvis that the world was waiting to see again. Elvis had returned to his roots.

When Claude choreographed the gospel segment of the show it required a lot of staging. Elvis became concerned about having to move and sing the lyrics to the long medley at the same time. With his backup singers, the much respected Blossoms—Jean King, Fanita James, and Darlene Love—singing live to track, Elvis asked if it would be possible to lip-synch the words and I told him that would be a big mistake. When we were at Western Recording Studios earlier doing the pre-record for the soundtrack, we had Elvis put the vocals on all the songs so it would help him memorize the lyrics. At first Elvis agreed with me on singing the words live, but when it came to the actual taping of the medley, he changed his mind and insisted he wanted to lip-synch.

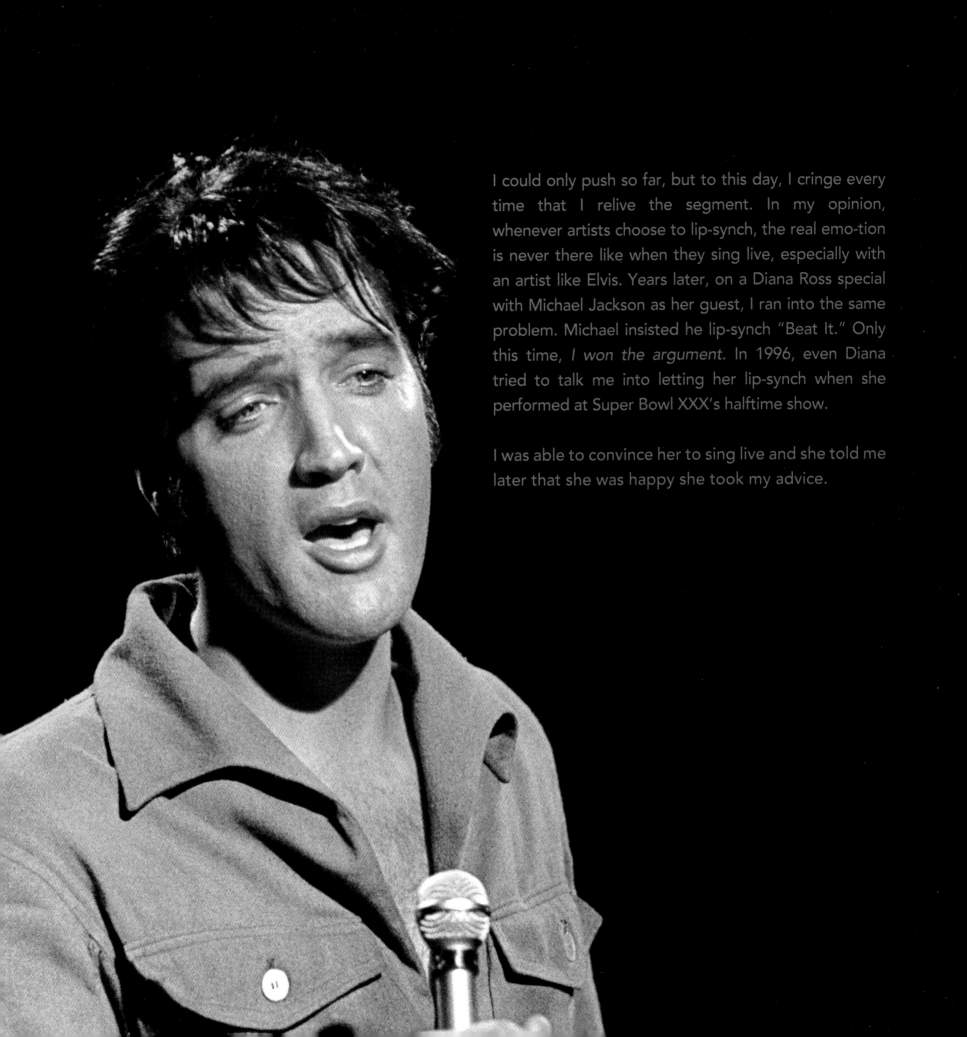

I could only push so far, but to this day, I cringe every time that I relive the segment. In my opinion, whenever artists choose to lip-synch, the real emo-tion is never there like when they sing live, especially with an artist like Elvis. Years later, on a Diana Ross special with Michael Jackson as her guest, I ran into the same problem. Michael insisted he lip-synch "Beat It." Only this time, *I won the argument*. In 1996, even Diana tried to talk me into letting her lip-synch when she performed at Super Bowl XXX's halftime show.

I was able to convince her to sing live and she told me later that she was happy she took my advice.

While preparing the special and going through hundreds of photographs of Elvis, I came across one of him sitting on his Harley Davidson motorcycle dressed in leather. It reminded me of Marlon Brando in *The Wild Ones*. I showed the picture to Bill Belew and asked if he could duplicate the outfit for Elvis for one of our segments. He told me that rather than copy the same store-bought clothes, he would like to design a special leather suit for Elvis to use in the show. I told him to go for it and we ended up using it twice, once in the arena segment and then again in the improv segment. What neither of us thought about at the time was how it would be for Elvis under those extremely hot theatrical lights. Elvis said, "Man, this thing's hot, I'm telling you" before singing "Love Me Tender" in the arena segment of the show.

One NBC executive, Dick Loeb, commented to me, "You can actually see sweat stains on his shirt under his armpits and you won't be able to show this in prime time television. You'll have to edit that out of the show."

Thank God they didn't get their way.

The nightly jam sessions continued even after long days of rehearsals. I for one knew I was watching an Elvis that his fans hadn't seen since 1954, when Sam Phillips, owner of Sun Records, recorded and released his first record "That's All Right." Elvis performed his first live concert that same year on July 17 at the Bon Air Club in Memphis with Scotty and bassist, Bill Black. What I was observing in that small dressing room was that original Elvis, raw and powerful, and it was all coming back to him. I knew that I had to tape this because no matter how clever we were in planning our rehearsed and scripted show, what I was seeing with no writers, no director, no sets or costumes involved, was the *real* Elvis.

I made the mistake of asking the Colonel if I could bring my camera into the dressing room and record what was going on. He smiled and said, "Definitely NO!"

Leaving me no alternative I then snuck in my Sony mini audiotape recorder, a pencil and pad and just started taking notes. I had to somehow change the Colonel's mind. Before I even had a chance to convince him, out of the blue, the Colonel told me that if I wanted to recreate what was happening in the dressing room, he'd let me do it on stage, but added that I'd be wasting my time. "Remember," he said, "this is only a one-hour Christmas special and there's no time to put this crap in." Recreating the dressing room jam sessions was definitely better than nothing at all, and I'd try to figure out how to use this material later.

"Steve just told us to go out there and have a good time—and we did. We had a ball out there."
—*DJ Fontana*

"I didn't realize until later that we actually did the first 'unplugged' session that came down the pipe."
—*Scotty Moore*

Left to right: Elvis, Charlie Hodge, Scotty Moore, Alan Fortas, and DJ Fontana

Left to right: Lance Legault, Elvis, and (with his back to camera) Charlie Hodge

"Seeing the '68 special on the big screen with a full audience at the Cinerama Dome in May 2008 brought back a lot of good memories. My favorite part of the special is the sitdown show—the *real* Elvis I knew comes through in that part of the show, jamming with friends, everyone just knowing what everyone else was doing. I'm so glad the special has lasted this long and drew an audience from all over the world. Scooch over puppies, the big dog's back in town."

—*Lance LeGault*

"I don't remember screaming—we were in the moment. I was listening to every word Elvis sang, didn't want to scream. I didn't want to miss a word of his singing."
—Joan Gansky, audience member

"Going to the taping was one of the most exciting things I have ever done as an Elvis fan. When he sang 'All Shook Up' Elvis looked right at me and I tried not to scream."
—Judy Palmer, audience member

The Colonel had still not given up on getting at least one Christmas song into the special. When I explained to Elvis what my plan was and how I was going to recreate what was going on in the dressing room, he insisted that he'd need Scotty Moore and DJ Fontana to do it with him. "There's not a guitar player in Hollywood that can play like Scotty," he said, and he tried to demonstrate to me on his guitar the "lick" that Scotty could play that he couldn't, and he felt that nobody else could either. I immediately organized their trip to Los Angeles. The wheels were in motion with the staff to prepare a special taping day for the dressing room sessions.

I decided to do two shows in one day with two completely different audiences. In a meeting with Bill Belew, he said he thought the black leather suit designed for the orchestra medley early on in the show would be appropriate. I insisted that there would be no amplifiers used in this segment so there wouldn't be any similarity or duplication between the orchestra segment and the improv segment. I told Gene McAvoy not to set up DJ's drum kit. He would have to play his drumsticks on Scotty's guitar case. We were all, by normal standards, crazy. I was flying by the seat of my pants and in 1968 an entire acoustic session had never been done—years before MTV or VH1 were even imagined. Rock musicians were used to turning their amplifiers up full throttle before blowing out the speakers.

But, this was Elvis, and I was willing to take chances, especially since I'd gotten this far and hadn't been fired yet!

When Allan and Chris received word that the improv segment was on, they immediately raced to their typewriters and banged out a script for Elvis to read. Of course, I had absolutely no intention of using it, because it would defeat the whole purpose of having Elvis do an improv segment. It would ruin an honest chance to look through that magic keyhole and see the real Elvis. This was the opportunity of a lifetime. But if you're curious to see what they wrote, here it is:

INFORMAL TALK AND SONGS: Have you ever thought what it's like to be an Elvis Presley? In the beginning when we were singing all those country songs back in Memphis, I never thought about it

much. Then one day we took the country and western sound and mixed it with a little colored soul, and all hell broke loose. People started to recognize me in the street . . . I've got to admit, I really got a kick out of that. Guys would just walk up to me and say, "Are you really Elvis Presley?" And I'd say, "Yeah." I'd stick my hand out to shake hands with 'em . . . they'd hit me right in the mouth and take off. That's when I knew I'd made it. Since then I've been put in the hospital thirty-seven times just for being Elvis Presley! I really got into trouble doing my "thing" in those days. In Los Angeles, I was told I had to stand still while performing . . . I couldn't touch my body with my hands in Philadelphia, and on network television, I couldn't be shot from the waist down. So this show is a real breakthrough for me. As you can see, I can now be shot from the waist down. (TAKE A SHOT) Pretty exciting, huh? I can touch my body with my hands (HE DOES) and I don't have to stand still while performing.

SINGS: "You Ain't Nothing But A Hound Dog" (HURTS HIMSELF—HOLDS SIDE) Well, that ain't as easy as it used to be I'll tell you! But that's all in the past. Being Elvis Presley today is a whole different bag. I've got the sideburns back because they're in again. But the three-inch pompadour is gone, along with the upper left lip scowl. Remember that? I did the entire production of Jailhouse Rock on that look alone, baby! I did a lot of movies and I've done a lot of songs in those movies. And here's a few toe-tappers that'll really knock your hat in the creek. You remember this one . . .

"My jewel kept falling out of my belly button and I remember Elvis patiently waiting, making cute little remarks between takes."

—Tanya Lomani, Little Egypt

MUSIC: "COTTON CANDY LAND" (ELVIS ONLY)

SANDMAN'S COMIN'
YES HE'S COMING
TO SPRINKLE YOU WITH SAND
HE'LL SAY ONE, TWO, TI IREE
AND YOU WILL BE
IN COTTON CANDY LAND

(SPEAKS)

And then there was . . .
MUSIC: "HOW WOULD YOU LIKE TO BE" (ELVIS ONLY)
HOW WOULD YOU LIKE TO BE
A LITTLE CIRCUS CLOWN
AND YOU COULD WEAR A SMILE
INSTEAD OF THAT FROWN
HOW WOULD YOU LIKE TO BE
A LITTLE KANGAROO
A-HOPPIN' UP AND DOWN
AND I COULD HOP WITH YOU
COME ON AND SMILE A LITTLE
SMILE A LITTLE
HOP A LITTLE, HOP A LITTLE
SMILE A LITTLE
HOP A LITTLE BIT WITH ME
SMILE A LITTLE, SMILE A LITTLE
HOP A LITTLE, HOP A LITTLE
SMILE A LITTLE, HOP A LITTLE
SMILE A LITTLE
HOP A LITTLE BIT WITH ME
OH HO AH HA

TRA LA LA LA LA LA LA
AH HA
TRA LA LA LA LA LA LA

(SPEAKS)

This one everybody seemed to like . . .
and so did I for a change!!

MUSIC:
"WOODEN HEART" (ELVIS ONLY)

CAN'T YOU SEE
I LOVE YOU
PLEASE DON'T BREAK
MY HEART IN TWO
THAT'S NOT HARD TO DO
CAUSE I DON'T
HAVE A WOODEN HEART
AND IF YOU SAY GOODBYE
THEN I KNOW
THAT I WOULD CRY
MAYBE I WOULD DIE
CAUSE I DON'T
HAVE A WOODEN HEART
THERE'S NO STRINGS UPON
THIS LOVE OF MINE

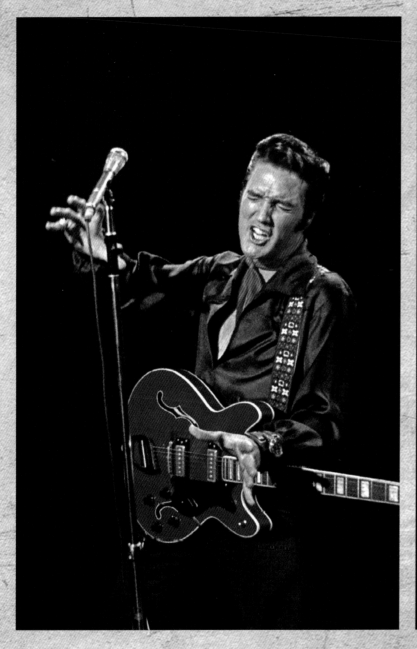
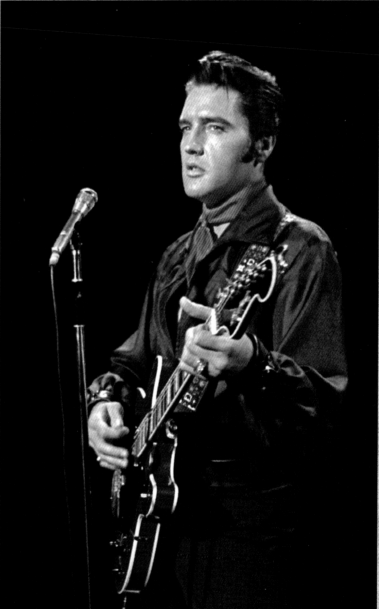

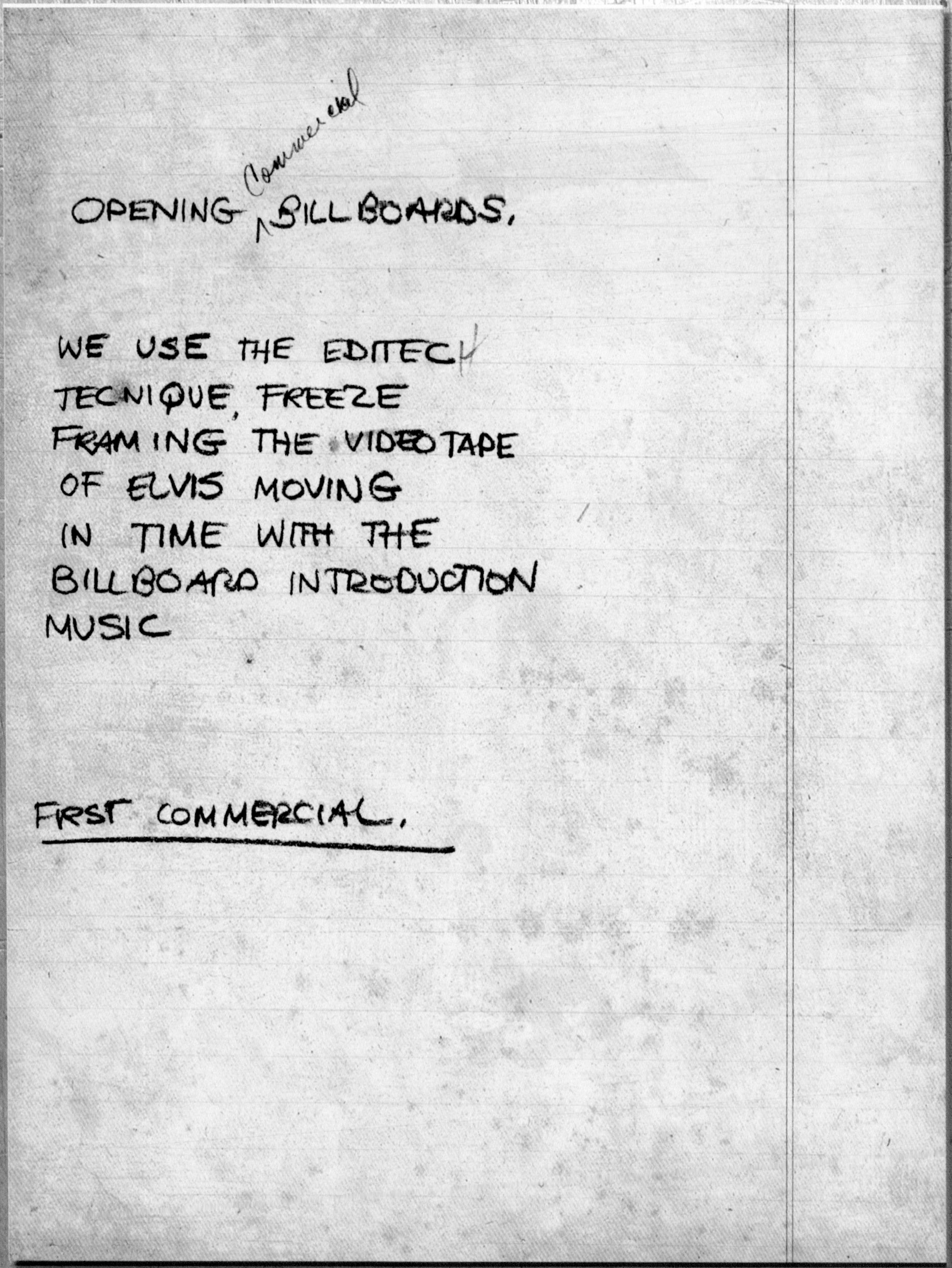

OPENING *Commercial* BILLBOARDS,

WE USE THE EDITECH
TECNIQUE, FREEZE
FRAMING THE VIDEOTAPE
OF ELVIS MOVING
IN TIME WITH THE
BILLBOARD INTRODUCTION
MUSIC

FIRST COMMERCIAL.

Steve Binder production note

IT WAS ALWAYS YOU
FROM THE START
TREAT ME NICE
TREAT ME GOOD
TREAT ME LIKE YOU REALLY SHOULD
CAUSE I'M NOT MADE OF WOOD
AND I DON'T HAVE
A WOODEN HEART
(GERMAN LYRICS TO COME)
THERE'S NO STRINGS UPON
THIS LOVE OF MINE
IT WAS ALWAYS YOU
FROM THE START
(GERMAN LYRICS TO COME)
CAUSE I DON'T
HAVE A WOODEN HEART

(SPEAKS)

Making movies is an experience that's hard to put into words. You know my movies. I'm usually the "goodie goodie" singing mechanic who always gets the girl. A lot of people ask me what I think of today's music. I'll never forget a couple of years ago, The Beatles came out to my house, and the first one I met was Ringo Starr. I said to him, "Are you really Ringo Starr?" He said, "Yeah, baby." I hit him right in the mouth! And Ringo said, "Now I know I really made it!" (LAUGH) I really like Beatle music, and a lot of the other music that's happening today. I like the way they sound, and I like what they're saying . . .

(INTO: "MEMORIES")

When I read their script, I felt like I do today when I watch a so-called reality show. Though the public may not realize it, most reality shows have writers and producers telling the people on the screen exactly what to do and say. To me, it's dishonest and the public deserves better.

When I scheduled the day and time to video the improvisational segment, I made the mistake of asking the Colonel if he needed any audience tickets for his personal friends. He looked at me funny, as if he had forgotten what segment I was talking about. He didn't think I was going to actually tape the segment even after he gave me his okay. He told me that if I wanted to see the real Elvis fans and not "your Hollywood phonies," I would have to give him all the tickets and he'd make sure the audience would be filled with Memphis teenagers with blue eyes and blonde bouffant hairdos. He would only accept all the tickets on one condition. No other tickets could be given to an NBC executive, sponsor, or my staff and crew.

I didn't have the authority to tell the executives or the sponsor's representatives that they couldn't come to the taping, so I immediately went to Bob Finkel again and explained the situation to him. I guess I was pretty convincing that if we did have the kind of audience the Colonel described to me, it would be nothing less than fantastic.

Finkel phoned me a few hours later and instructed me to give all the tickets to the Colonel and he would handle NBC and the sponsors. It came as a shock to the Colonel when I handed him all the tickets. I visualized this giant airplane flying out of Memphis with hundreds of pure and unadulterated Elvis Presley fanatics champing at the bit to see their idol close up and live on stage. Wouldn't you think the same? The night before the actual taping, I called a meeting with the guest relations department to warn them about crowd control in the morning. We agreed on adding additional NBC ushers and even spoke of contacting the Burbank police department if the crowd got rowdy. It seemed that I had covered all the bases, except what turned out to be the most important one.

Driving off the lot that evening, the guard on duty at the gate asked me if I needed any tickets for tomorrow's *ELVIS* show. At first I took it as a joke until I saw a huge stack of our tickets sitting on the desk inside the shack. I couldn't believe my eyes. But even then I didn't panic. It never entered my mind that the Colonel's goal was to sabotage the segment.

I could barely sleep that night in anticipation for what was about to happen. I received a phone call early the next morning from the executive in charge of guest relations and all ushers.

I was advised that I had better get to the studio as soon as I could because there was nobody showing up to see the *ELVIS* show and one of the lead ushers had put on extra staff to handle the crowd. I dressed quickly, headed to Burbank to see with my own eyes what was happening outside the studio. We were scheduled to start taping two shows in the afternoon. When I arrived at the studio, a few people were starting to collect outside on Alameda Street, so I still wasn't panicking. As soon as I walked in the door, I was told that the people I saw were probably the extra pages hired to handle the overflow audiences.

It was then it sunk in and I realized the Colonel had duped me.

There was to be no airplane filled with screaming teenagers from Tennessee to see Elvis in person. The Colonel had merely given all the tickets to the NBC gate guards or likely thrown many of the tickets away. I panicked. Bones said he'd phone a few radio disc jockeys in Los Angeles that he knew personally and have them ask their audience to drive to the NBC Burbank Studios if they wanted to see Elvis in person.

We sent our people to the famous Bob's Big Boy, a drive-in restaurant close to NBC known for its hamburgers with special sauce and malted milkshakes, to invite them to see Elvis in person when they finished their lunch.

When it came time to tape, we had gathered an audience made up of friends, relatives, and employees that were available to come to Stage 4. Moments before I was about to roll tape, my stage manager told me that Elvis asked to see me and his voice told me that it was not good news. I found Elvis in the makeup room. When I entered, he asked the woman applying his makeup to leave. Elvis said that it was not that he wasn't willing to go out there, but his mind was a total blank. He didn't remember anything he said or sang in the dressing room and felt he shouldn't go out on stage. Everything had all gone away.

Trying to hold my composure, I found a piece of blank paper and in the next few minutes scribbled down from memory what stories he told and what songs he sang that I remembered and in no time filled up a page and handed it to him.

I shoved the paper into his hand, looked him straight in the eye, and said calmly, "Elvis, do this for me! If you get out there and really can't think of anything to say or sing, then say hello and goodbye to the audience and come on back...but you've got to go out there!"

I turned around, not looking back to see the expression on his face, and headed for the control room to give the command to roll tape. Scotty, DJ, Charlie Hodge, and Alan Fortas were already on the small stage seated on blue leather and metal chairs. Bassist Chuck Berghofer was placed off camera and Lance LeGault, with tambourine in hand, was below the stage next to where Elvis would be sitting, prepared to hand up any of Elvis's many guitars.

The Colonel was placing what he thought were the prettiest girls on the steps of the stage close to where Elvis would be sitting while Robert W. Morgan, a local disc jockey from KHJ Radio, was warming up the audience. The stage was fifteen feet square and painted red, white, and black. The spillover audience was seated in bleachers surrounding the stage. "Get them close to Elvis," the Colonel barked. "Who here really loves Elvis?" You'd think that the Colonel's carnival and sideshow were about to begin, but fortunately and instead, the improvisation segment turned into one of the greatest comebacks in show business history. The lights dimmed and we heard the roar of the crowd starting to swell. I had my fingers crossed that it would somehow work out well. "Please God," I said to myself, and then as if my prayer was answered, there he was. Elvis Presley, finding his way back home.

He worked his way through the crowd, climbing the steps to his awaiting chair and just stood there for what seemed like an eternity taking in the crowd before he picked up his guitar. I was fascinated just watching him look at the audience. He smiled, sat down, and started talking. He thanked the audience for coming and joked about not knowing what he was supposed to do. He even pretended to fall asleep. But the minute he picked up his guitar and started to sing "That's All Right," I knew I could finally relax. His lifeblood oozed out of every pore in his body. He never sat still in that chair. He squirmed on it like the seat was covered with ants. It was like the evening jam sessions in the dressing room, only now Elvis was the sweaty, sexy, fertility god, dressed in black leather that matched the color of his boots and jet black hair. "Mah Boy! Mah Boy!" he repeated over and over again knowing he was home. *Elvis Presley was back to reclaim his crown as the King of Rock 'n' Roll.*

Days earlier, when Elvis was afraid he wouldn't know how to end the improvisation taping in front of a live audience, we devised a signal that when I sensed it was over, I would cue the track to "Memories," a new song submitted and written by Mac Davis and Billy Strange. Before Elvis committed to singing their song, he came to me and asked if I would help him rewrite one or two of the lines. The original line had the words "bubblegum" and "cotton candy" in it and he didn't want to sing those words. I can't remember the line that we replaced it with, but it obviously made him happy. He would wrap up the end of the song he was singing, walk through the audience of young women seated around him, and come downstage to the steps.

I gave him no direction once he was there. I felt he would know what to do. I think "Memories" was the perfect ending to the session, and it made the charts as another Elvis Presley hit record immediately after the special aired. When the first taping was completed, we took a break to bring in everyone who had found out what was going on and wanted to get a peek at Elvis. We also found Elvis a guitar strap, and put a rug on the floor of the stage to dampen the sound of all of their stomping boots.

Now there are a lot of rumors circulating that when Elvis came backstage after the first session, he was dripping with sweat from the hot lights. When Bill Belew went to dry his leather shirt and pants, he discovered that Elvis had an orgasm during his performance. All I can remember is Bill, running up to me with the pants in hand, showing me the caking stain and asking me what he should do to remove the semen from the inside of the pants. Bill was freaking out because he didn't know if there would be enough time to dry the pants before the next session. He gathered up his wardrobe staff and all the hair dryers he could find to get the job done. I learned another "director" lesson at that moment: to never make just one set of clothes for any star. Always have a duplicate or even three of everything, just in case (providing the main costume is not too expensive). To my knowledge, though, it never happened again.

On the very first airing on NBC, the entire one-hour show length was cut to approximately forty-eight minutes of programming content, in order to accommodate the commercials and station breaks, so I was forced to use only the improvisation material as short introductions to the production segments like the gospel and other segments.

It wasn't until HBO bought the entire improvisation segment from RCA and the Elvis Presley Estate and renamed the show *One Night with You* that it caught the public's full attention.

When Elvis died on August 16, 1977, NBC rushed to air a three-hour tribute special. For the very first time, my ninety-minute show was broadcast, this time with the bordello segment reinserted.

From then on, the original one-hour show was buried and basically forgotten . . . and only the ninety-minute version is now shown worldwide.

Elvis with the Blossoms: Jean King, Fanita James, and Darlene Love

"Elvis could be shy and introverted, but when it came to gospel music he opened up."
—Darlene Love, the Blossoms

"People would be shocked to know how hard he worked on this special."
—*Jaime Rogers, Choreography*

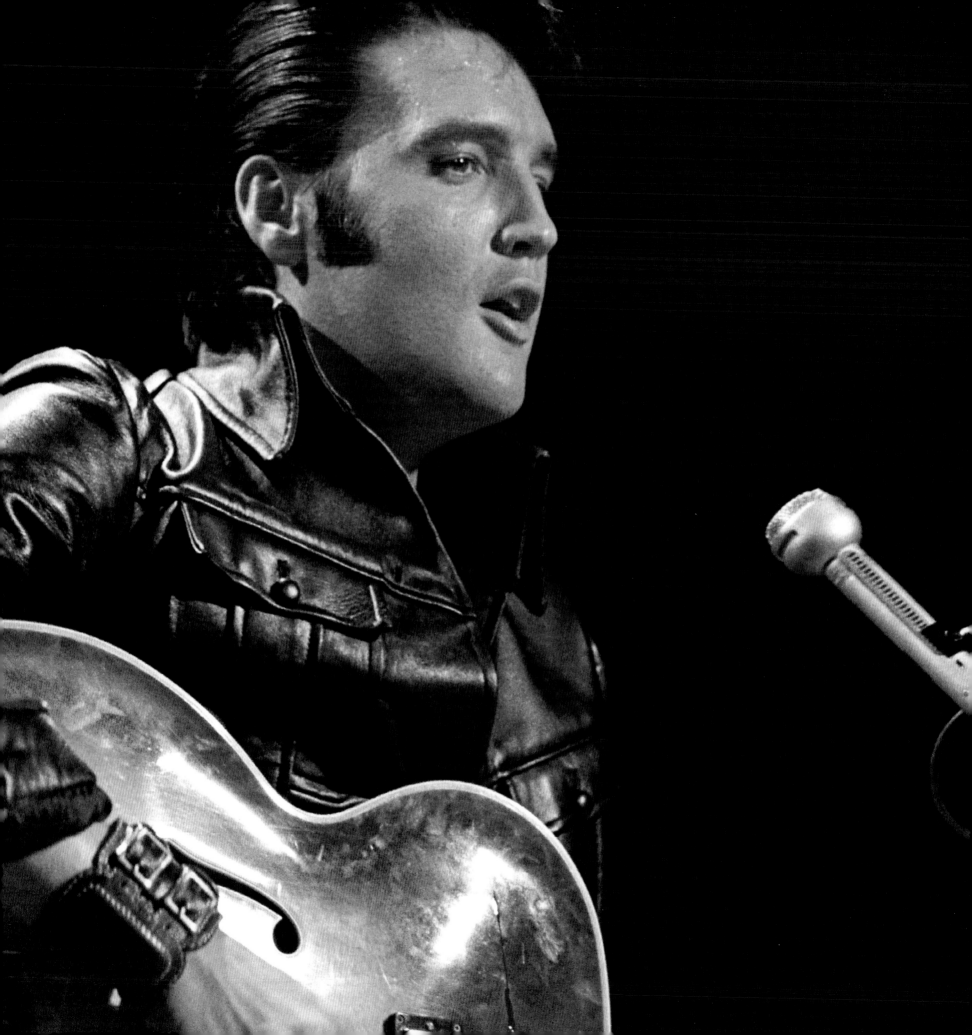

"The special was a natural extension of all our talents coming together at the same time."
—*Chris Beard, Writer*

"When we first met with Steve he told us all they want is an Elvis Christmas special and we said, "What do you need us for then?"
—*Allan Blye, Writer*

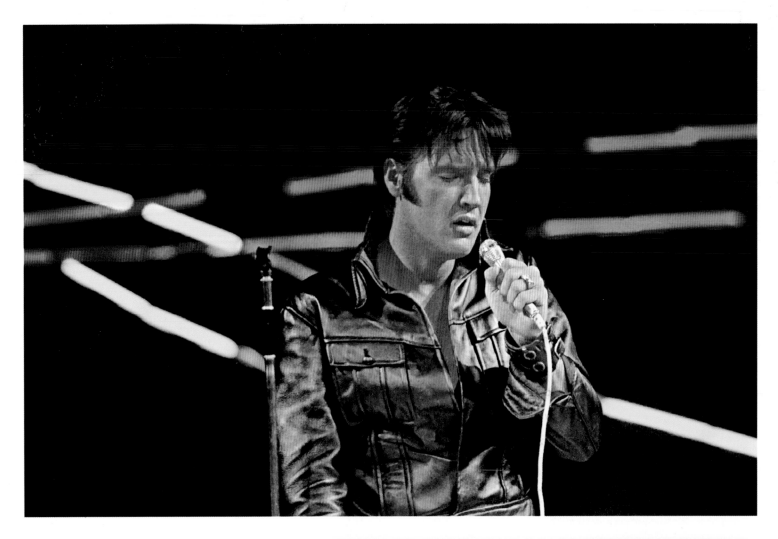

"When I designed the boxing ring, I wanted to show the crowd was all around him, breathing on him. Elvis had the animal quality— always prowling around the stage."
—Gene McAvoy, Art Direction

"Then I did the '68 special with Elvis and I gotta tell ya man, I listened to that every once in a while, and I played my ass off on that thing."
—Hal Blaine, Drummer

OFFICIAL
ELVIS
PRESLEY
SHOW

WESTERN RECORDERS

Some of the most exciting hours spent with Elvis were at the pre-recording sessions from June 20–23 at Western Recorders, located at 6000 Sunset Boulevard, Hollywood.

Western Recorders had a long history of being the place to record music because of their state-of-the-art facilities and recording expertise. I can personally remember going to a session there earlier to watch Frank Sinatra record one of his great albums. Bones was using Western to record many of his hit records with the 5th Dimension and the Association. It wasn't easy convincing NBC to record there. Early on when we announced to NBC that we were hiring freelance musicians and going to an outside facility to record, they typically resisted. Word came down that it would cost too much money—why couldn't we use the same musicians that Bob Hope used on his specials and record at NBC? I seriously doubt if there were any of Bob Hope's orchestra under the age of forty or outside the jazz era. Bones and I knew that wouldn't work for Elvis, so we set out to get the best rock 'n' roll musicians we could fi nd and stood our ground. The musicians we used would later become The Wrecking Crew.

When Elvis walked into Studio 1 at Western Recorders, he saw the greatest West Coast musicians ready to play on the soundtrack of his special, including some of the best studio rhythm men in the entire world: Hal Blaine and Johnny Cyr on drums and percussion; Don Randi on piano and organ; Chuck Berghofer on bass and keyboard; Mike Deasy, Al Casey, and Tommy Tedesco on guitar; and Larry Knechtel on keyboards.

Elvis took one look inside the studio and panicked. He called me out onto Sunset Boulevard and made me promise that if he didn't like the sound of the orchestra, I would send them all home with the exception of the rhythm section. It occurred to me that Elvis hadn't even heard a Billy Goldenberg arrangement and was going strictly on my word that he would be great.

To my surprise, he confessed to me that he had never sung with anything larger than a rhythm section consisting of no more than a guitar, bass, and drums. He told me that he didn't even know if he would know how to sing with such a big orchestra. Reluctantly, I gave him my word that I would send all of the musicians home and keep the rhythm section but *only* on the condition that he give it a try.

We walked back into the studio of waiting musicians and Elvis stepped up alongside Goldenberg, who was standing on his conductor's two-foot riser above the orchestra. They nodded at one another and Billy gave the downbeat to "Guitar Man." Need I say more? The recording sessions were a blast. Tommy Morgan was sensational playing the harmonica and all the musicians were having the time of their lives. On a coffee break, I remember overhearing Mike Deasy and Tommy Tedesco fooling around and creating a scratching sound on their guitars. I loved what I heard. I went to Bones and asked that after the coffee break we record about two minutes of them scratching away and I used the sound on "Guitar Man" as an underscore to the main opening and end titles. I still love that sound.

COLONEL PARKER

When I first met Colonel Parker, I tried to show him respect. After all, his reputation as Elvis's manager was unquestioned by people who did business with him. But as the days and weeks went by, I quickly came to realize that he was a childish bully who took advantage of other people's weaknesses. Parker was the wizard depicted in one of my favorite movies, *The Wizard of Oz*. He was the actor, Frank Morgan, hiding behind black curtains with lots of gadgets and colored lights, connected to nothing. His hollering and threats were hollow and only worked on people who wanted something from him. I realized early on that there was absolutely nothing he possessed that could be used as leverage to get me to do what he ordered me to do, even if it meant my being fired—and he knew it. That's exactly why he was so frustrated. For the time we were making the '68 special, the Colonel's power over Elvis was nowhere to be found.

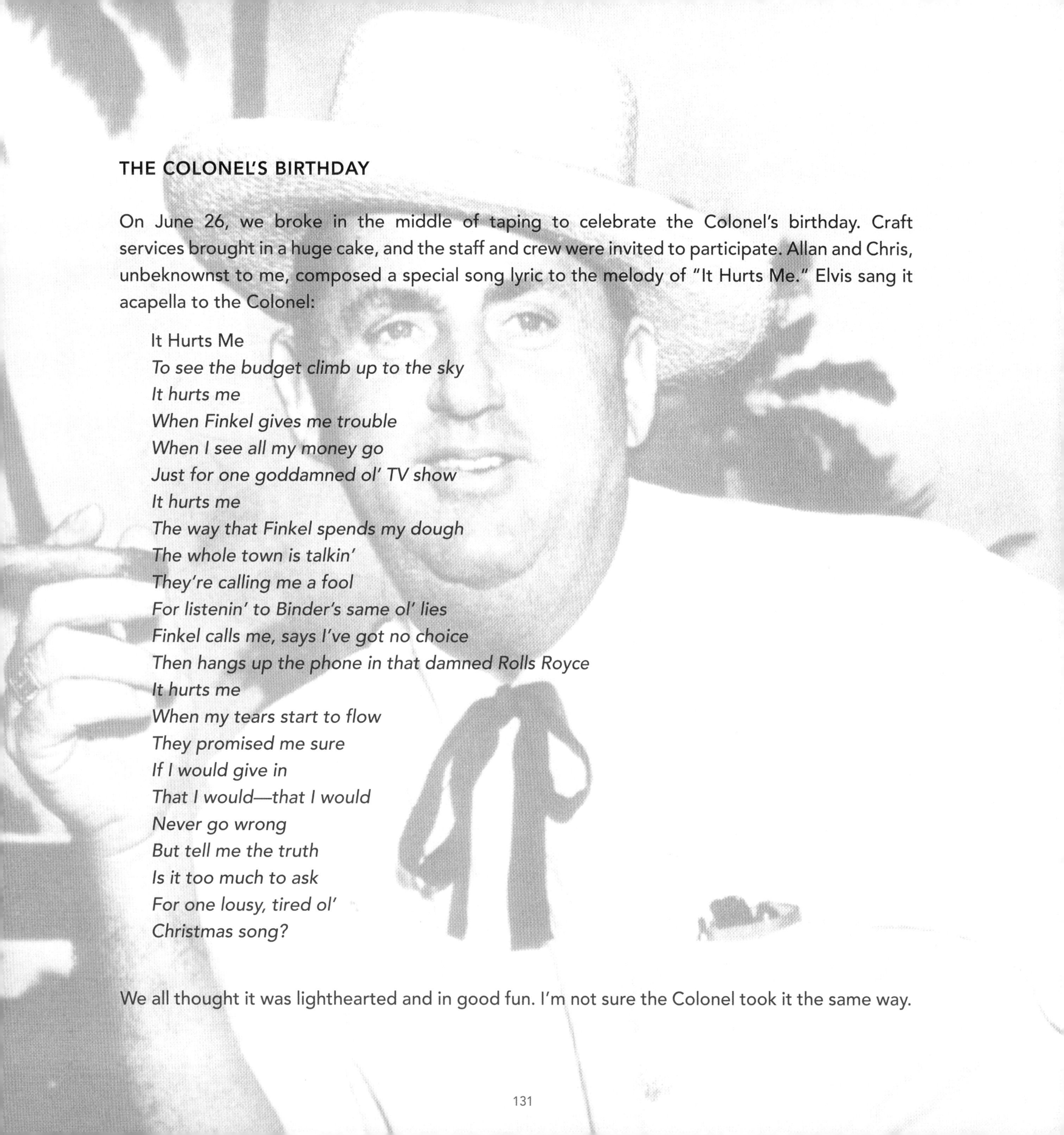

THE COLONEL'S BIRTHDAY

On June 26, we broke in the middle of taping to celebrate the Colonel's birthday. Craft services brought in a huge cake, and the staff and crew were invited to participate. Allan and Chris, unbeknownst to me, composed a special song lyric to the melody of "It Hurts Me." Elvis sang it acapella to the Colonel:

It Hurts Me
To see the budget climb up to the sky
It hurts me
When Finkel gives me trouble
When I see all my money go
Just for one goddamned ol' TV show
It hurts me
The way that Finkel spends my dough
The whole town is talkin'
They're calling me a fool
For listenin' to Binder's same ol' lies
Finkel calls me, says I've got no choice
Then hangs up the phone in that damned Rolls Royce
It hurts me
When my tears start to flow
They promised me sure
If I would give in
That I would—that I would
Never go wrong
But tell me the truth
Is it too much to ask
For one lousy, tired ol'
Christmas song?

We all thought it was lighthearted and in good fun. I'm not sure the Colonel took it the same way.

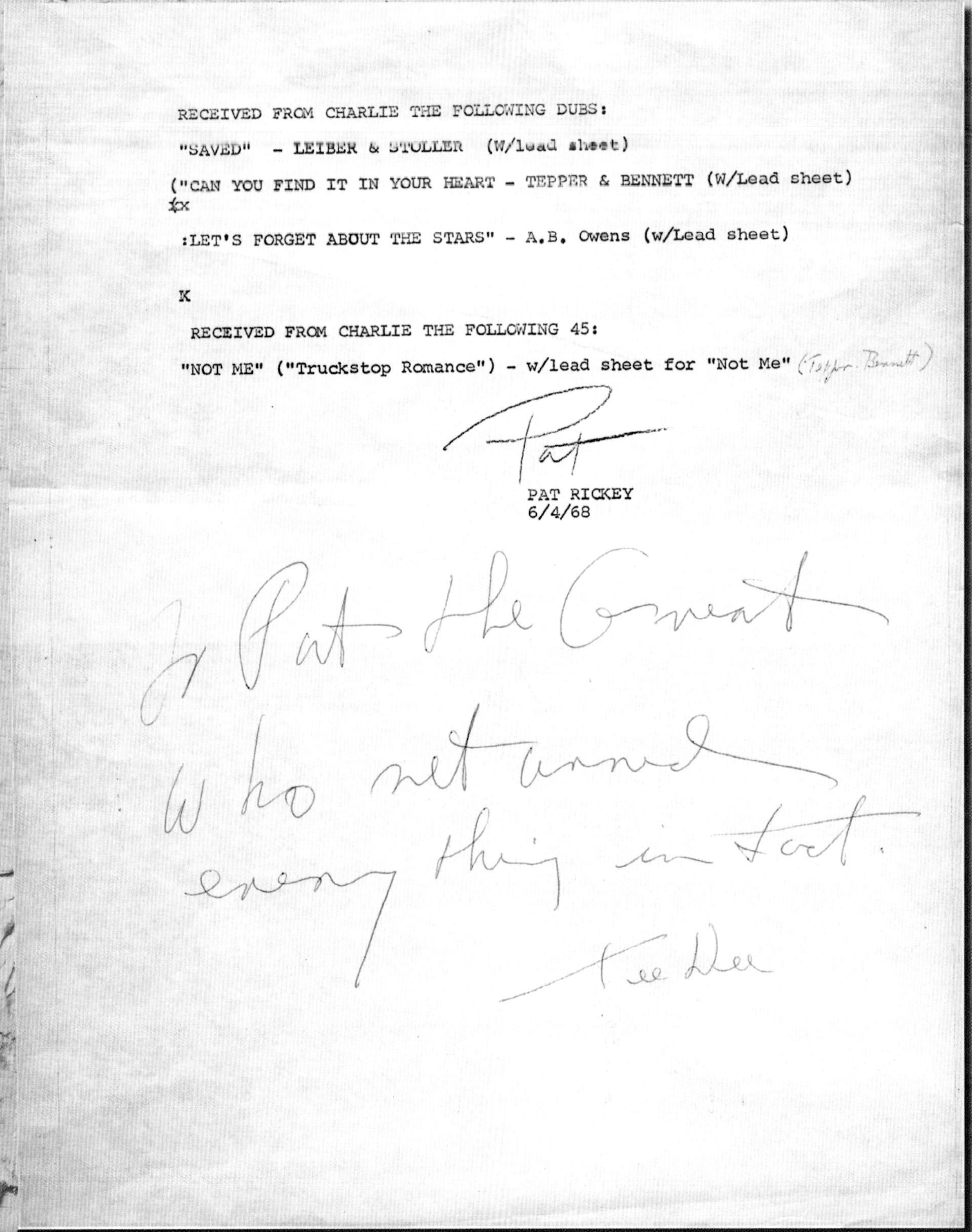

RECEIVED FROM CHARLIE THE FOLLOWING DUBS:

"SAVED" - LEIBER & STOLLER (W/lead sheet)

("CAN YOU FIND IT IN YOUR HEART - TEPPER & BENNETT (W/Lead sheet)
xx

:LET'S FORGET ABOUT THE STARS" - A.B. Owens (w/Lead sheet)

K

RECEIVED FROM CHARLIE THE FOLLOWING 45:

"NOT ME" ("Truckstop Romance") - w/lead sheet for "Not Me" *(Tepper-Bennett)*

Pat

PAT RICKEY
6/4/68

*To Pat the Great
Who set around
everything in fact.

Tee Dee*

Despite the handwritten notation (Tepper - Bennett) beside "Not Me" ("Truckstop Romance"), these songs were not written
by Sid Tepper and Ray C. Bennett. "Not Me" was written by Jerry Leiber, Mike Stoller, and Billy Edd Wheeler.
"Truckstop Romance" was witten by Billy Edd Wheeler.
Both of these songs were recorded by Bill Edd (Wheeler) and released on United Artists 517.

June 17, 1968

Colonel Tom Parker
Elvis Exploitations
MGM Studios
10202 West Washington Blvd.
Culver City, California 90230

Dear Colonel Parker:

Would you request from MGM a release of the master
tape of "A Little Less Conversation." We would like
their permission to use this master tape for the
Elvis Presley Special, to be aired December 3, 1968.
We also would like a composite minus Elvis' voice so
that he can sing live to the track on the show.

                              Sincerely,

                              STEVE BINDER
                              Producer

SB:lm

c.c: Mr. Bob Finkel

Steve Binder and Elvis on the first night of recording at Western Recorders

Photos at Western Recording Studios on Sunset Boulevard courtesy of George Rodriquez

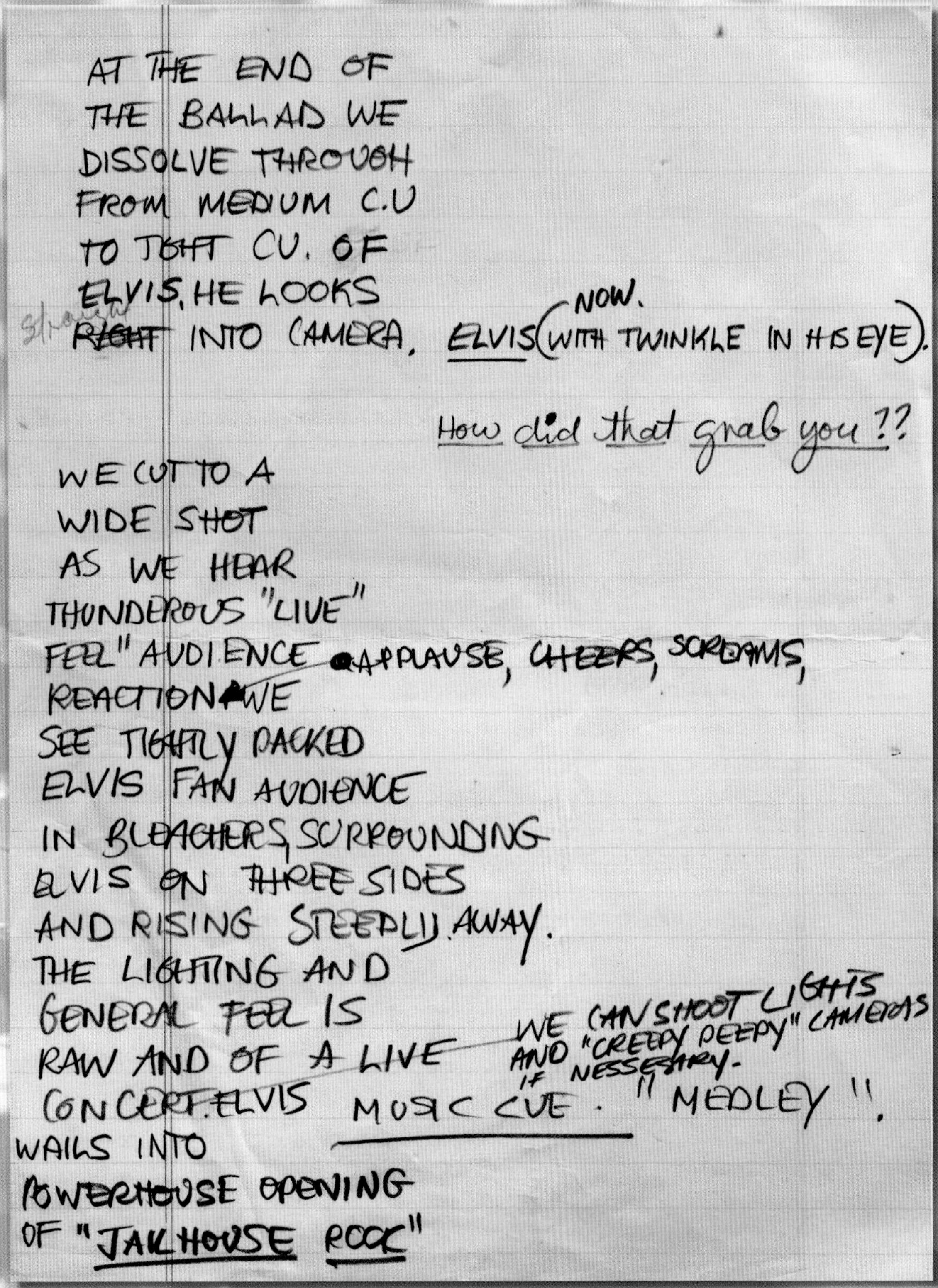

AT THE END OF
THE BALLAD WE
DISSOLVE THROUGH
FROM MEDIUM C.U
TO TIGHT C.U. OF
ELVIS. HE LOOKS
~~RIGHT~~ _{SQUARE} INTO CAMERA. <u>ELVIS</u> NOW. (WITH TWINKLE IN HIS EYE).

<u>How did that grab you</u> ??

WE CUT TO A
WIDE SHOT
AS WE HEAR
THUNDEROUS "LIVE"
FEEL" AUDIENCE @APPLAUSE, CHEERS, SCREAMS,
REACTION AWE
SEE TIGHTLY PACKED
ELVIS FAN AUDIENCE
IN BLEACHERS, SURROUNDING
ELVIS ON THREE SIDES
AND RISING STEEPLY AWAY.
THE LIGHTING AND
GENERAL FEEL IS
RAW AND OF A LIVE   WE CAN SHOOT LIGHTS
                        AND "CREEPY PEEPY" CAMERAS
                        IF NESSESARY.
CONCERT. ELVIS   MUSIC CUE . "MEDLEY".
WAILS INTO   _____
POWERHOUSE OPENING
OF "<u>JAILHOUSE ROCK</u>"

Western Recorders, left to right: Bones Howe, Steve Binder, and legendary drummer, Hal Blaine

Bones Howe at the console and Steve Binder consulting with script supervisor Pat Rickey

Knowing that the closing song of the special had to make a personal statement about Elvis and knowing that time to fi nd it was running out, I asked Billy Goldenberg and Earl Brown to go home and write a song that would express who Elvis was. An Elvis who was thrown into the spotlight and who seemed to really care about the world around him.

Our television "family" came from all walks of life, all religions, all races, but had one thing in common. We worked in television and wanted to do the best job we knew how using the most powerful medium in the world to say something not only entertaining, but meaningful. Earl and Billy promised me that they would give it a shot. Not long after, Earl phoned me at home to tell me that he and Billy had written the song I requested and were anxious to play it for me.

We agreed to meet an hour before taping started the next morning. When I arrived at the studio Earl and Billy were already waiting for me. We went into the empty piano room in Elvis's dressing room and they proceeded to sing to me "If I Can Dream." Billy played the upright piano and Earl sang, "If I can dream of a better land, where all my brothers walk hand in hand . . ." I asked them to play it again and by that time I was convinced that I had found my closing song. When Elvis walked into his large dressing room that morning, I motioned for him to follow me into the other room. At the same time, the Colonel and his entourage held court there.

I asked Elvis to sit next to Billy on the piano bench while Earl sang "If I Can Dream" to him. Elvis listened, but gave no reaction. He asked them to sing it two or three more times without letting on to us whether he liked it. He just sat there listening. I could hear the Colonel's voice through the paper-thin door shouting "over my dead body" and "they're wasting valuable time in there."

Elvis looked at me and said, "I'll do it, I'll sing the song on the show." And with that, the door separating the two rooms burst open and in came the Colonel, Tom Diskin, and Freddie Bienstock with a contract and pen in hand for Billy and Earl to sign, giving away all the rights to their publishing to Hill & Range. The Colonel, with Tom Diskin at his side, didn't want another open confrontation with me since he obviously anticipated and knew that Elvis had already said yes.

The Colonel was biting his stogie and fuming. Billy Goldenberg graciously said that Earl had really written the song all by himself and removed his name from the lead sheet. The Colonel had lost his final battle . . . or so it seemed . . . until another big battle was fought with the Colonel and myself over inserting a Christmas song into the special after I had completed editing and delivered the final master tape to NBC without any Christmas songs in it.

That kind gesture by Billy Goldenberg, erasing his name from "If I Can Dream" cost him a small fortune. The songwriter splits the royalties with the publisher 50-50. Since the album soundtrack from his 1968 Comeback Special began Elvis's recording career resurgence, the monies received by Earl Brown were enormous. Billy Goldenberg, by the stroke of his eraser, cost himself half of Earl's share. That's what I call integrity!

Bones Howe and I arranged for all of our musicians to return to Western Recorders so we could lay down the track to our new closing song. Even though I planned to have Elvis sing live to the track of "If I Can Dream," the story of that memorable day remains with me like it happened yesterday.

After the orchestra played the last note of the day and the musicians packed up their instruments and headed out the door, Elvis came to me and asked if he could put his vocal on the track to practice with since he wasn't that familiar with the lyrics. I informed Bones and the recording engineer what was about to happen and we locked the door to the studio and set up for Elvis to record once again. The only people left in the studio were Elvis, Bones, and Pat Rickey (my script supervisor), a recording engineer, his utility man, and me. It was getting late in the evening, and we had been working steadily since very early that morning.

The boom microphone was set up in the middle of the stage and Elvis put his headset on so he could listen to the track while he sang. His voice boomed: "I'm ready, Bones, you can roll the tape," and Bones did. Elvis sang the lyrics and we all thought we were going home knowing his vocal was never going to be used other than for Elvis's use.

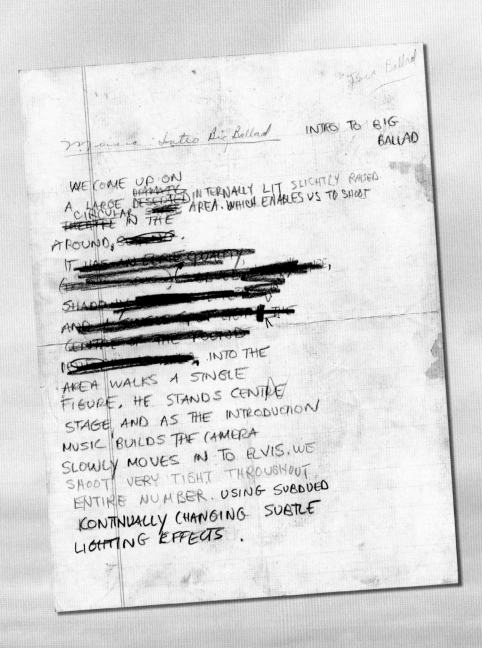

Just as I was about to say good night to Elvis on the intercom, his voice boomed out again. "I'd like to try it one more time if you don't mind, but this time with a hand mic." I don't think anyone else but Elvis ever made such a request, singing a vocal in a recording studio on a hand mic. Bones gave the word to his utility engineer, and we were about to begin.

At the last minute, I asked that all the lights be turned out in the large and now empty studio.

The only lights left on were the panel lights on Bones's mixing board, the little red lights on the musicians' amplifiers, and the lights on the tape meters and tape machines reflecting on the glass separating the control room from the stage. It set an eerie mood. Looking out from the control booth glass into the studio, I could barely see the outline of Elvis standing in front of all the empty musicians chairs and music stands.

Bones started the tape playback and as Elvis started to sing, he dropped to the studio floor in a fetal position, clutching the microphone close to his mouth, and seemed oblivious to his surroundings—and us. What surprised me at the time was that Elvis had already memorized most of the words. It was all that basic instinct coming out through his entire being and forming the words to the song as they escaped his throat. It was raw and powerful . . . animal-like.

If only I had had a camera at the time!

As great a performance as it was to an audience of five, I still made the decision to have him sing live to the track when we taped "If I Can Dream" at NBC. I admit that the television taping came nowhere close to his performance at the recording studio, but I still stand by my decision to have him sing live rather than lip-synch on television.

"I was by the camera when Elvis sang my song 'If I Can Dream' and I was thinking, 'God, is this as great as I think it is?'"
—Earl Brown, Lyrics and Vocal Arrangements

When I went into editing and saw all the great improv segments, I said, "This is the show. I've got to get a lot of this material in." So when I finished editing I had completed a ninty-minute version. I phoned Finkel and told him what I had done and asked if it would be possible to open up another thirty minutes of airtime. He laughed and promised he'd try but didn't really hold out any hope for that to happen. The show's sponsor, Singer, flatly refused and I was forced to remove what I considered to be the heart of the show, the improvisation segment. The sixty-minute version that originally aired on NBC had only brief snippets of the improv used only as interstitial glue for the production segments.

On August 16, I delivered all the masters and outtakes to NBC. A few days later, after the Colonel had seen a screening of the special, I was ordered into a meeting with Tom Sarnoff and Herb Schlosser (president of NBC at the time). When I walked through the glass door heading to Herb Schlosser's office, the Colonel was already sitting there, leaning on his cane.

During the entire meeting, he never took his steel blue eyes off of me. I actually had the strange feeling he was trying to hypnotize me. Schlosser told me that the Colonel was extremely unhappy and called attention to the fact that there was no Christmas song in the show. The Colonel informed him that he wouldn't allow NBC to air the show without one. Silence prevailed while they waited for an answer from me. With the full knowledge that I never shot any Christmas songs except Elvis singing "Blue Christmas" in one of the improv segments, I said that I could pull out one of the other songs in the show and put "Blue Christmas" in its place. The entire time I spoke I stared right back at the Colonel. The Colonel told Schlosser that he was satisfied with my solution since all he really cared about from the beginning was saving face.

Ironically, a year later, on August 17, 1969, NBC rebroadcast *ELVIS* and replaced "Blue Christmas" with "Tiger Man."

When I completed editing the sixty-minute version of the show with my editors Wayne Kenworth and Armond Poitras, I set up a screening for Elvis in one of NBC's small projection rooms. It was a dark room with about fifteen theater seats. Elvis showed up with the usual suspects: Jerry Schilling, Joe Esposito, Charlie Hodge, Lamar Hunt, and Alan Fortas. I invited a few key members of my staff. During the screening, it was hard not to stare at Elvis to see his reactions to the show. He appeared to me to be pretty relaxed and, on occasion, laughed at himself in the right spots.

When the lights went up, Elvis asked if he could see it again but this time without all the people in the screening room, except for me. I was sure he was holding back while they were there and now wanted to tell me what he wanted taken out or changed before the show aired.

All of my insecurities came to the surface. As soon as I finish my final edit on any project, I always fall into a funk. I guess it's because I'm so high while I'm directing, with all my adrenaline flowing, that when everything suddenly stops, I crash. I hate waiting to hear what other people, even the star, have to say about my work. There are times when I don't want to even look at my work. Some shows that I've produced and directed that I personally felt missed their mark have brought me great acclaim in the industry while others that I thought I did my best work in have been most criticized.

All I ever cared about was the respect and love of the people I worked with.

While the two-inch tape was being rewound, I stepped outside the room and made plans to meet everybody after the final screening at Bill Belew's apartment for some laughs, beer, and pizza.

Elvis backstage with Earl Brown and Gene McAvoy

When I walked back into the room, Elvis was sitting there anxious for me to start the show again. He asked me what we were talking about outside, and I told him about our beer and pizza party at Bill's apartment. I asked him to come along and join us.

He smiled and thanked me for the invitation, but declined. I asked the tape operator to turn the speakers up to their maximum volume and to roll the tape for the second time. During the screening, Elvis would lean over to me time and again to say how much he loved what he was looking at. This time he wasn't holding back.

His laughs were louder and his enthusiasm was contagious. It was like he couldn't believe his own eyes. When it was over and the lights came up, he told me how proud he was of the show and *how glad he was that he had trusted me.*

Then he got in one of his quiet moods. I could tell that he was thinking hard. He told me that because of the newfound "freedom" (his exact word) he experienced, he would never again make a movie or sing a song that he didn't believe in.

I told him that as much as I wanted to believe him, I wasn't sure he was strong enough. I told him that the first thing he had to do was take control of his life, even if that meant breaking away from the Colonel. He looked at me, broke out into one of his infectious laughs, and said, "Okay, I'll go."

At first I didn't know what he meant, until he asked if he could drive with me, and the boys would follow us in his Lincoln Continental. Now do you know how exciting it was to drive in a little yellow Ford convertible with Elvis sitting by my side? The entire time I worked with him I felt like an equal and he was never anything more than a man. But now, sitting beside him in the front seat of my open convertible, with my then-wife Judi in the backseat, driving past the world-famous Hollywood Bowl on Highland Boulevard and watching the reactions of passersby as they recognized Elvis, it felt different.

No longer was I a fellow worker, but an Elvis Presley fan. Bill, Earl, Gene, and Billy had already left an hour earlier to get the beer and pizza. I should have called them, but I didn't want to stop at a pay phone in the midst of heavy traffic. Elvis was having a ball. He was waving at the people in the cars surrounding us and talking, especially to the girls. I loved being part of the whole scene.

When we pulled up in front of Bill's apartment, Elvis shoved a piece of paper into my hand, closed my fist, and said, "Don't tell anyone I gave this to you." I asked why and he said, "That's the only way you'll be able to talk to me." The Lincoln behind us emptied and we all walked up the stairs to Bill's apartment. I rang the doorbell. It was dead quiet. I rang again. Nothing. One look at Elvis's face told me how disappointed he was. We just stood there for a minute, though it seemed like an eternity to me. And then someone suggested we go downstairs and use the car phone in the Lincoln. In those days, owning even a car phone was a rarity. We headed downstairs for the car and Elvis asked me for Bill's number as Joe Esposito dialed it. We couldn't reach anyone on the phone. Elvis said to me, "We'll do it another time Steve, but thanks for asking me. Oh, and don't forget what I gave you."

Elvis and the gang piled into their car and as they were driving off and turning the corner, I couldn't help but remember the night of the improvisation session when I wasn't sure Elvis was even going to come out on stage. This time all my prayers for Bill and the guys to be home went unanswered. Later I found out that the guys were still out buying pizza and beer and we missed them by minutes. When I tried calling Elvis a few days later at the number he handed to me, a strange voice answered the phone and told me I had the wrong number.

That evening, in front of Bill's apartment in Hollywood, turned out to be the very last time that I would ever speak to Elvis.

BIG BALLAD.

ORIGINAL BIG BALLAD
(WORDS TO COME)

POST-SPECIAL

ELVIS was first broadcast at 9:00 p.m. on Tuesday, December 3, 1968. On December 4, when the ratings were released, NBC reported that *ELVIS* captured 42 percent of the total viewing audience. It was the network's biggest rating victory for the entire year and the season's top-rated show.

The ninety-minute version of the special would not be seen by the public until November 20, 1977, after Elvis's death, when NBC rushed to air a three-hour tribute special titled *Memories of Elvis* hosted by Ann-Margret. It combined *Aloha from Hawaii* with the '68 special. By sheer accident, someone new at NBC charged with retrieving the master tape of the special grabbed the ninety-minute version—not realizing this was not the show that aired in 1968. Truthfully, I thought they had erased it or destroyed it, but obviously they hadn't.

When Elvis opened at the International Hotel in Las Vegas, I went to see him at my own expense and he was fantastic. I made an attempt to go backstage to say hello and congratulate him, but the security guard at the hotel said he couldn't reach anyone when he phoned Elvis's dressing room to announce me.

Years later, Joe Esposito told me that if he had known I was there, he'd have come down and brought me upstairs personally. To this day I've never accepted Joe's explanation.

I always felt that the Colonel had put out the word right after the special aired that I was persona non grata and Elvis was never told that I was downstairs. I had that same feeling earlier when I tried phoning Elvis using the number on the paper he had put in my hand in front of Bill Belew's apartment in Hollywood. I'm sure that Elvis never gave me the wrong phone number. It appeared to me that Elvis was a prisoner in his own house and was *sneaking* a message to the outside world.

When Billy Goldenberg was hired to score an Elvis movie, *Change of Habit*, the same movie the Colonel offered me to direct at the very beginning and was part of the Colonel's deal with NBC and National General Pictures, Billy Goldenberg contacted me on several occasions to say that Elvis was always asking about me and wondering how I was getting along.

A year or so later, I went back to Las Vegas and made it a point to see his show at the hotel Elvis was performing at.

I knew right then that it was over. How sad I felt for him.

Elvis was now only a shell of the man that I was fortunate enough to know. He was now performing for his musicians instead of the audience that paid to see him. I knew he was bored and his heart was no longer into performing. The man that I knew wanted to climb new mountains. He wanted to meet his fans from all over the world in their countries and discover new and exciting things. It never came to pass. With all the theories surrounding Elvis's death, I've always felt that Elvis died of boredom, not drugs. For the King of Rock 'n' Roll to end his life and career as nothing more than a saloon singer in Las Vegas was definitely not the way I would have liked to see him go out.

The Colonel had his final victory. An empty and shameful one at that.

IF I CAN DREAM

There must be lights burning brighter somewhere
Got to be birds flying higher in a sky more blue
If I can dream of a better land
Where all my brothers walk hand in hand
Tell me why, oh why, oh why can't my dream come true
There must be peace and understanding sometime
Strong winds of promise that will blow away

All the doubt and fear
If I can dream of a warmer sun
Where hope keeps shining on everyone
Tell me why, oh why, oh why won't that sun appear

We're lost in a cloud
With too much rain
We're trapped in a world
That's troubled with pain
But as long as a man
Has the strength to dream
He can redeem his soul and fly
Deep in my heart there's a trembling question
Still I am sure that the answer gonna come somehow
Out there in the dark, there's a beckoning candle

And while I can think, while I can talk
While I can stand, while I can walk
While I can dream, please let my dream
Come true, right now
Let it come true right now
Oh yeah

Words and music by W. Earl Brown

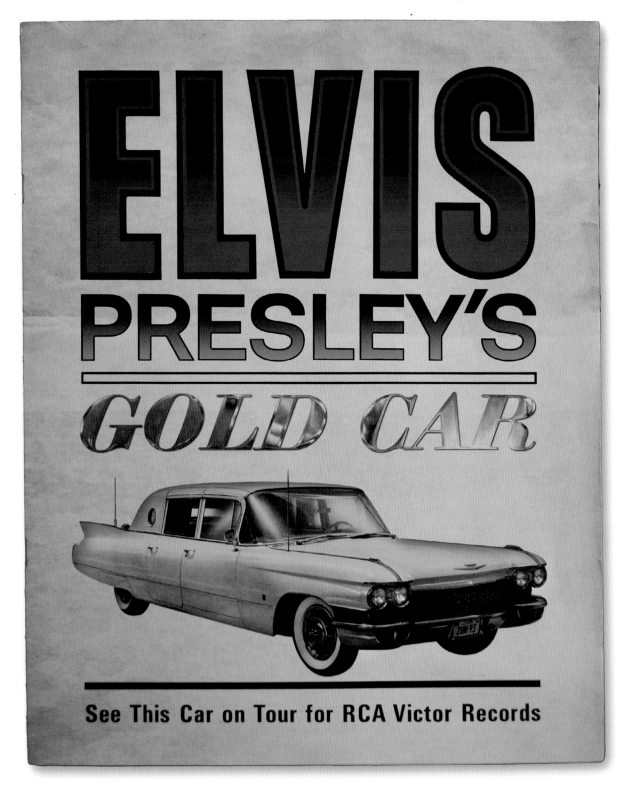

Rare commercial poster of Elvis Presley's gold Cadillac by General Motors.

RECORDING SESSIONS

Location
WESTERN RECORDERS, BURBANK, CALIFORNIA

JUNE 20, 1968
Nothingville / Guitar Man (part 1) (guitar man section 1)
Let Yourself Go (part 1 / guitar man section 2)
Let Yourself Go (part 1 / female vocal overdub)
Flicker Routine / Let Yourself Go (part 2)
Let Yourself Go (part 3)
Alley Pickup (guitar man section 3)
Let Yourself Go (composite)
Guitar Man (part 2 - fast / escape section 1)
Amusement Pier Music (escape section 2)
Big Boss Man (escape section 3)
It Hurts Me (part 1 / escape section 4)

JUNE 21, 1968
Guitar Man (part 2 - slow / escape section 1 remake)
It Hurts Me (part 2 / after karate section 1)
It Hurts Me (composite)
Guitar Man (part 3) / **Little Egypt** (after karate section 2)
Trouble / Guitar Man (part 4 / after karate section 3)
Road Medley (composite)
Sometimes I Feel Like a Motherless Child
Where Could I Go But to The Lord
Up above My Head - intro (gospel section 1)

JUNE 22, 1968
Up above My Head / I Found That Light / Saved
Intro (gospel section 2)
Saved (part 1) / **Preach for the Sky / Saved** (part 2)
(gospel section 3)
Gospel Medley (composite)
Trouble (opening)
Guitar Man (opening)

JUNE 23, 1968
Karate Musical Interlude (instrumental)
The Scratch (instrumental)
If I Can Dream
If I Can Dream (dubdown to rhythm track)
Memories (rhythm track)
Let Yourself Go (closing instrumental)
A Little Less Conversation (rhythm track)

JUNE 24, 1968
Mono and stereo mixing session

JUNE 24, 1968
Memories (vocal overdub)
A Little Less Conversation (vocal overdub)
Let's Forget about the Stars (not attempted)
Can You Find It in Your Heart (not attempted)
Not Me / Truckstop Romance (not attempted)

Musicians

Guitar: Tommy Tedesco
Guitar: Michael Deasy, Al Casey
Bass / keyboards: Larry Knechtal
Bass: Charles Berghofer
Piano: Don Randi
Drums: Hal Blaine
Percussion: John Cyr, Elliot Franks
Bongos: Frank DeVito
Harmonica: Tommy Morgan
Keyboard: Bob Alberti
Keyboard: Tommy Wolfe

Backup Vocalists

The Blossoms: Darlene Love, Jean King, Fanita James
Julie Rinker, B.J. Baker, Frank Howren, Bill Lee, Gene Merlino,
Thurl Ravenscroft, Bill Brown, Joe Eich, Elaine Back,
Dean Parker, Jack Gruberman, Sally Stevens, Jackie Ward,
Ronald Hicklin, Tom Bahler, and Mitch Gordon

Orchestra

Conductor: Billy Goldenberg
Arrangers: Billy Goldenberg, Jack Elliot
Violin: Leonard Atkins; Leonard Malarsky, Sidney Sharp,
Thelma Beach, Marvin Limonick
Piano: Marvin Limonick, Joseph Stepansky, Alexander Murray,
Ambrose Russo
Cello: Eleanor Saltkin, Paul Bergstrom, Christine Walevska,
Emmett Sargeant, Richard Noel, Frank Rosolino, Ernest Tack
Trombone: Francis Howard
Trumpet: Oliver Mitchell, John Audino, Manny Stevens,
Anthony Terran
Saxophone: Anthony Ortega, Peter Christlies, John Kelso,
Gene Cipriano
French horn: Dick Perrisi, William Hinshaw

Location

ELVIS PRESLEY'S DRESSING ROOM, NBC /
BURBANK STUDIO, BURBANK, CALIFORNIA

JUNE 24, 1968

I Got A Woman
Blue Moon / Young Love / (The Sun Is Shining)
Oh Happy Day
When It Rains It Really Pours
Blue Christmas
Are You Lonesome Tonight? / That's My Desire
That's When Your Heartaches Begin
Love Me
When My Blue Moon Turns to Gold Again
Blue Christmas
Santa Claus Is Back in Town

JUNE 25, 1968

Danny Boy
Baby What You Want Me to Do
Love Me
Tiger Man
Santa Claus is Back in Town
Lawdy Miss Clawdy
One Night
Blue Christmas
Baby What You Want Me to Do
When My Blue Moon Turns to Gold Again
Blue Moon of Kentucky

Musicians

Acoustic guitar / electric guitar: Elvis Presley
Acoustic guitar / electric guitar: Scotty Moore
Acoustic guitar: Charlie Hodge
Percussion: D.J. Fontana, Alan Fortas
Tambourine: Lance Legault

Location
NBC / BURBANK STUDIO, BURBANK, CALIFORNIA

JUNE 25, 1968
Press conference held

Location
NBC / BURBANK STUDIO, BURBANK, CALIFORNIA

JUNE 27, 1968 (VIDEOTAPED)
Big Boss Man (amusement pier part 10)
It Hurts Me (amusement pier part 2)
It Hurts Me (amusement pier part 2 pickups)
It Hurts Me (partial overdub)

JUNE 27, 1968 - Warm-up rehearsal*
That's All Right
Heartbreak Hotel
Love Me
Baby What You Want Me to Do
Blue Suede Shoes
Lawdy Miss Clawdy
Are You Lonesome Tonight?
Santa Claus is Back in Town
When My Blue Moon Turns to Gold Again
One Night
Memories

Musicians
Acoustic guitar / electric guitar: Elvis Presley
Acoustic guitar / electric Guitar: Scotty Moore
Acoustic guitar: Charlie Hodge
Percussion: D.J. Fontana
Percussion: Alan Fortas

* It is presumed that this rehearsal was not recorded on audio or videotape

JUNE 27, 1968 (VIDEOTAPED) - 6:00 p.m. improv segment
That's All Right
Heartbreak Hotel
Love Me
Baby What You Want Me to Do
Blue Suede Shoes
Baby What You Want Me to Do
Lawdy Miss Clawdy
Are You Lonesome Tonight?
When My Blue Moon Turns to Gold Again
Blue Christmas
Trying to Get to You
One Night
Baby What You Want Me to Do
One Night
Memories (singing to pre-recorded rhythm track)

JUNE 27, 1968 (VIDEOTAPED) -
8:00 p.m. improv segment
Heartbreak Hotel
Baby What You Want Me to Do

Introductions
That's All Right
Are You Lonesome Tonight?
Baby What You Want Me to Do
Blue Suede Shoes
One Night
Love Me
Trying to Get to You
Lawdy Miss Clawdy
Santa Claus is Back in Town
Blue Christmas
Tiger Man
When My Blue Moon Turns to Gold Again
Memories (singing to pre-recorded rhythm track)

```
                    (PARODY - "IT HURTS ME")                    Earl Brown
                                                                    and
                                                                Allan Blye
IT HURTS ME

TO SEE THE BUDGET CLIMB UP TO THE SKY

IT HURTS ME

WHEN BINDLE GIVES ME TROUBLE

WHEN I SEE ALL MY MONEY GO

JUST FOR ONE GOD-DAMNED OL' TV SHOW

IT HURTS ME

THE WAY THAT BINKEL SPENDS MY DOUGH


THE WHOLE TOWN IS TALKIN'

THEY'RE CALLIN' ME A FOOL

FOR LISTENIN' TO BYNDER'S SAME OL' LIES

FINKEL CALLS ME, SAYS I'VE GOT NO CHOICE

THEN HANGS UP THE PHONE IN THAT DAMNED ROLLS ROYCE

IT HURTS ME

WHEN MY TEARS START TO FLOW


THEY PROMISED ME SURE

IF I WOULD GIVE IN

THAT I WOULD - THAT I WOULD

NEVER GO WRONG

BUT TELL ME THE TRUTH

IS IT TOO MUCH TO ASK

FOR ONE LOUSY, TIRED OL'

CHRISTMAS SONG...?
```

June 26, 1968: Elvis took a break during the special to celebrate Colonel Parker's birthday party with photo of Executive Producer Bob "Napoleon" Finkel and to sing the parody of "It Hurts Me" to the NBC executives.

Musicians

Acoustic guitar / electric guitar: Elvis Presley
Acoustic guitar / electric guitar: Scotty Moore
Acoustic guitar: Charlie Hodge
Percussion: D.J. Fontana
Percussion: Alan Fortas
Tambourine: Lance Legault

JUNE 28, 1968 (VIDEOTAPED)
Sometimes I Feel Like A Motherless Child /
Where Could I Go But To The Lord / Up above My Head
Up above My Head / Saved
Saved (part 2 pickups)
Saved (part 3 pickups)
Let Yourself Go (bordello part 1)
Let Yourself Go (bordello part 2)
Let Yourself Go (bordello part 3)
Bordello (insert)
Bordello (part 2, no Elvis)

JUNE 29, 1968 (VIDEOTAPED) - 6:00 p.m. arena segment
Heartbreak Hotel (incomplete)
One Night (incomplete)
Heartbreak Hotel
Hound Dog
All Shook Up
Can't Help Falling in Love
Jailhouse Rock
Don't Be Cruel
Blue Suede Shoes
Love Me Tender

Trouble / Guitar Man*
Baby What You Want Me to Do
If I Can Dream (lip-synched performance)

JUNE 29, 1968 (VIDEOTAPED) - 8:00 p.m. arena segment
Heartbreak Hotel
Hound Dog
All Shook Up
Can't Help Falling in Love
Jailhouse Rock
Don't Be Cruel
Blue Suede Shoes
Love Me Tender
Trouble (false start)*
Trouble (false start)*
Trouble / Guitar Man (incomplete)*
Trouble / Guitar Man (reprise)*
Trouble / Guitar Man (reprise)*
If I Can Dream (lip-synched performance)

Musicians

Electric guitar: Elvis Presley
Guitar: Tommy Tedesco
Guitar: Michael Deasy
Guitar: Al Casey
Bass / keyboards: Larry Knechtal
Bass: Charles Berghofer
Piano: Don Randi
Drums: Hal Blaine
Percussion: John Cyr
Percussion: Elliot Franks
Bongos: Frank DeVito
Harmonica: Tommy Morgan

Backup Vocalists

The Blossoms: Darlene Love, Jean King,
Fanita James, Julie Rinker, B.J. Baker,
Frank Howren, Bill Lee,Gene Merlino,
Thurl Ravenscroft, Bill Brown, Joe Eich,
Elaine Back, Dean Parker, Jack Gruberman,
Sally Stevens,Jackie Ward, Ronald Hicklin,
Tom Bahler, and Mitch Gordon

JUNE 30, 1968 (VIDEOTAPED)

Nothingville (road #1)
Guitar Man (road #1 vocal overdub)
Guitar Man (road #2 vocal overdub)
Guitar Man (road #3 vocal overdub)
Huh-huh-huh (promo)
If I Can Dream (vocal overdub)
Trouble (opening overdub) /
Guitar Man (opening playback)
Guitar Man (alley, vocal overdub)
Little Egypt / Trouble (nightclub, vocal overdub)
Trouble (discotheque, vocal overdub)
Trouble (supper club vocal overdub)

Closing Credits

Orchestra

Conductor: Billy Goldenberg
Arrangers: Billy Goldenberg; Jack Elliot
Violin: Leonard Atkins, Leonard Malarsky, Sidney Sharp;
Thelma Beach; Marvin Limonick
Piano: Marvin Limonick; Joseph Stepansky; Alexander Murray,
Ambrose Russo
Cello: Eleanor Saltkin, Paul Bergstrom, Christine Walevska,
Emmett Sargeant, Richard Noel, Frank Rosolino, Ernest Tack
Trombone: Francis Howard
Trumpet: Oliver Mitchell, John Audino, Manny Stevens,
Anthony Terran
Saxophone: Anthony Ortega, Peter Christlies, John Kelso,
Gene Cipriano
French horn: Dick Perrisi, William Hinshaw

June 23, 1968, Western Recorders with guitarists Tommy Tedesco and Michael Deasy

SUMMARY LAYOUT SHEET
Page 1

DECEMBER 1968 - VICTOR LP RELEASE
(Ships - Immediately)

LPM-4088 "ELVIS"   LIST CATEGORY - LPM - $4.79
Side 1
WPRM-8051 "NEW ORTHOPHONIC" HIGH FIDELITY P8S-1391 ELVIS.DEC 1968release

** 1- TROUBLE   TP3-1008   3:26 *   WPA1-8030   Elvis Presley Music
       (Leiber-Stoller)   Inc., BMI
       GUITAR MAN TP3-1008   *   WPA1-8047   Vector Music Corp.,
                                                      BMI
    2- LAWDY, MISS CLAWDY TP3-1008*   WPA1-8031   Venice Music Inc.,
       (Lloyd Price)   BMI
       BABY, WHAT YOU WANT ME TO DO*   WPA1-8032   Conrad Music, BMI
       (Reed)
       DIALOGUE TP3-1008
       Medley: TP3-1008
       a. HEARTBREAK HOTEL   *   WPA1-8083   a.Tree Music, BMI
          (Axton-Durden-Presley)
       b. HOUND DOG   *   WPA1-8034   b.Elvis Presley
          (Leiber-Stoller)   Music Inc., & Lion
       c. ALL SHOOK UP TP3-1008   *   Pub. Co. Inc. BMI
          (Blackwell-Presley)   WPA1-8035   c.Elvis Presley
       CAN'T HELP FALLING IN LOVE *   WPA1-8036   Music Inc.,& Travis
       (Weiss-Peretti-Creatore)   Music Co., BMI
       JAILHOUSE ROCK   TP3-1008*   WPA1-3037   d.Gladys Music Inc.,
       (Leiber-Stoller)   ASCAP
       DIALOGUE   e.Elvis Presley
       LOVE ME TENDER TP3-1008   Music Inc., BMI
       (Presley-Matson)   f.Elvis Presley
    (from the Original Sound Track Of his NBC-TV   Music Inc., BMI
                                  SPECIAL)
                 Elvis Presley   ##J.Leiber & M.
    *TAPES PURCHASED FROM NBC   Stoller, BMI
    RECORDING DATES NOT AVAILABLE

    **Recorded in stereo

        TP3-1008 ELVIS.....APRIL 1969 RELEASE

                                    LISTING

                                    DEC 9 1968

                                    ORIGINAL COPY

SUMMARY LAYOUT SHEET
Page 2

DECEMBER 1968VICTOR LP RELEASE
(Ships-Immediately)   LIST CATEGORY - LPM -$4.79

LPM-4088   "ELVIS"   P8S-1391 ELVIS..DEC 1968 RELEASE
Side 2
WRPM-8052

** 1-DIALOGUE   Affiliated Music
    WHERE COULD I GO BUT TO THE LORD* WPA1-8039 Enterprises,Inc.,BMI
                    TP3-1008
      (J.B.Coats)   WPA1-8040 Gladys Music Inc.,
      UP ABOVE MY HEAD   ASCAP
      (W.Earl Brown) TP3-1008
      SAVED   WPA1-8041 Progressive Music Pub.
      (Leiber-Stoller)   7:25   Co. Inc. & Trio
                                                 Bibo Music Pub.,
    2-DIALOGUE TP3-1008   WPA1-8042 Inc. ASCAP
    +BLUE CHRISTMAS
      (Hayes-Johnson)   WPA1-8043 Elvis Presley Music
      DIALOGUE   *   Inc., & Travis Music
      ONE NIGHT   Co., BMI
      (Bartholomew-King)   5:37
                                      WPA1-8044 Gladys Music Inc.,
    #3-MEMORIES TP3-1008 3:18 *   ASCAP
      (Strange-Davis)
                                      WPA1-8045 a. Gladys Music Inc.,
    ** 4-Medley: TP3-1008   6:42 *   ASCAP
       a. NOTHINTVILLE
          (Strange-Davis)   WPA1-8046 b. Ludix Pub. Co. &
       DIALOGUE   TP3-1008 *   Conrad Music, BMI
       b. BIG BOSS MAN   WPA1-8047 c. Vector Music Corp.,
          (Smith-Dixon)   *
       c. Guitar Man   WPA1-8048 d. Elvis Presley
          (Jerry Hubbard)   *   Music Inc., & Trio
       d. LITTLE EGYPT   WPA1-8030 Music Co. Inc., &
          (Leiber-Stoller)   *   Progressive Music Pub.
       e. TROUBLE   WPA1-8047 Co. Inc., BMI
          (Leiber-Stoller)   *   e. Elvis Presley
       f. GUITAR MAN   Music Inc., BMI
          (Jerry Hubbard)   WPA1-8029 f. Vector Music Corp.,
    *5-IF I CAN DREAM TP3-1008 3:16 *   BMI
      (W.Earl Brown)   5. Gladys Music
                                                 Inc.,ASCAP
             TP3-1008 ELVIS
    (from the Original Soundtrack of his NBC-TV Special
                 Elvis Presley
    *TAPES PURCHASED FROM NBC   LISTING
    RECORDING DATES NOT AVAILABLE   DEC 9 1968
                                               ORIGINAL COPY
    **Recorded in stereo

          + CPL8 - 3699
         # CPL1 - 1349
        # CPL 2 - 4031   FINAL

Left to right: Priscilla Presley, Steve Binder, and Bones Howe
at the Paley Film Festival celebrating the 40th anniversary of the Elvis special

Left to right: Steve Binder, Bones Howe, Allan Blye, Lance Legault, and Chris Bearde
also attending the Paley Film Festival

'ELVIS'

Elvis Presley in a musical special. Executive producer Bob Finkel. Producer-director Steve Binder, writers Allan Blye, Chris Beard. Musical production Bones Howe. Musical direction and arrangements William Goldenberg. Special lyrics and vocal arrangements Earl Brown. Choreography Jamie Rogers, Claude Thompson. NBC, Tuesday, 9 p.m.

The Elvis hour on NBC was virtually a one-man show with the star doing most of his numbers on a small square stage surrounded by a studio audience which had some screamers in it. But according to executive producer Bob Finkel, none of them were hand-picked. They just simply loved Elvis.

Although he didn't indulge in the dynamic physical gyrations which made him so controversial that we saw only the top half of him on an Ed Sullivan Show many years ago, Elvis still generates considerable heat with his singing.

His repertoire included many of his recorded hits such as "Hound Dog," "Jailhouse Rock" and "Love Me Tender." Producer-director Steve Binder employed lots of camera closeups and two-camera superimposed shots, which were effective, except for those closeups showing Elvis sweating. I don't think many viewers care to see singers sweat on TV.

Moving away from the small stage and studio audience, Elvis did two impressive production numbers. One was a gospel song with dancers and singers; the other opened on a carnival midway and progressed from his singing in a joint to better-class night-clubs.

The show closed with him in a white suit standing in front of the huge lit letters spelling E-L-V-I-S which opened the proceedings, and he sang "If I Can Dream."

Except for TV runs of his old movies, this marked Elvis' first TV appearance since he did a guest shot on a Frank Sinatra special in 1960, so it was an event in that sense and Elvis managed to sustain the hour very well.

THANK YOU . . . THANK YOU VERY MUCH

I for one choose to remember the Elvis that I intimately got to know in 1968 and not the sequined version that he became known for just a few years later. I like to think that Elvis felt the same way that I did about the making of the '68 special.

It was extraordinary to be part of the magic that came from Elvis and his original duo, Scotty Moore and DJ Fontana, who played together on our special for the very last time. Fortunately for all of us, the heart, soul, and music of Elvis continue to inspire millions around the world each and every year.

I am convinced that there will never be another Elvis.

He was definitely a one and only.

I am so thankful that fate intervened 50 years ago, allowing me to play a small role in his life and music history.

NATIONAL BROADCASTING C

NBC COLOR CITY

3000 W. ALAMEDA AVE., BURBANK

363

"ELVIS"

starring

ELVIS PRESLEY

IN COLOR

Children Under 12 Will Not Be Admitted